WHAT THEY BRING

The Poetry of Migration and Immigration

WHAT THEY BRING

The **Poetry** of **Migration** and **Immigration**

Edited and with an Introduction by
Irene Willis and Jim Haba

IPBOOKS.net
International Psychoanalytic Books

International Psychoanalytic Books (IPBooks)
New York
IPBooks.net

International Psychoanalytic Books (IPBooks),
47–46 40th Street, #3E
Sunnyside, NY 11104
Online at: www.IPBooks.net

Cover painting: Erica Barton Haba
Jazz Stripes No. 21
Acrylic on paper, 20 x 17 in., 2010

Cover and interior book design by Blackthorn Studio

ISBN: 978-1-949093-53-7

To Erica Barton Haba and
to the memory of Bernard Daves Rossell (d. 2016)

About the Authors

Irene Willis has published five full-length poetry collections, plus an anthology of poems called *Climate of Opinion: Sigmund Freud in Poetry* (IPBooks, 2017). Three times nominated for Pushcart Prizes and once for a National Book Award, her poems have also appeared in many journals and anthologies. She has received a Distinguished Artist Fellowship from the New Jersey State Council on the Arts, a residency fellowship from the Millay Colony for the Arts and grants from the Massachusetts Arts Council and the Berkshire/Taconic Foundation. She holds a B.S. from SUNY Fredonia, M.A. and Ph.D. from New York University and M.F.A. in Poetry from New England College. A longtime educator, she has taught in high schools, colleges and graduate schools, most recently at Westfield State University and American International College, both in Massachusetts. Currently she is Poetry Editor of an online publication, www.internationalpsychoanalysis. net, where she has a monthly column, "Poetry Monday." She is a member of the Authors' Guild and an Educator Associate of the International Psychoanalytic Association.

Jim Haba is well-known in the poetry world as poet, editor and teacher at Rutgers University and Rowan University but is even better-known for his work organizing large poetry events and working to bring poets and poetry to national audiences. The Founding Director of the biennial Dodge Poetry Festival in New Jersey, the largest poetry event in North America, he also created and developed the Dodge Foundation's Poetry in the Schools program, which brings poets directly into high schools to work with students and teachers. Readers may know him best as the editor of Bill Moyers' best-selling poetry book, *The Language of Life*, and television viewers for three series of PBS poetry programs he made with Moyers. In 2000 Jim Haba was presented with the Elizabeth Kray Award, given annually by Poets House to a member of the poetry community for distinguished contributions to the art. In 2011 he received the *Paterson Literary Review* award for Lifetime Service to Poetry. He has had numerous other awards for his work, and in 2006 published two new chapbooks. Also a fine artist, whose ceramic tile murals and painted-paper collages are in collections throughout the United States, he studied at the Studio School in New York City and holds a B.A. from Reed College and a Ph.D. from Cornell University.

"let the oppressed go free;
share your bread with the hungry
and take the wretched poor
into your home."

–Isaiah

"Whoever degrades another degrades me,
and whatever is done or said returns at last to me."

—Walt Whitman

Table of Contents

Introduction

I remember how excited I was, at about seven or eight, to learn Pig Latin, because if I said it fast enough it could sound like the babble of a foreign language, which was what I heard, growing up in various neighborhoods on the west side of Manhattan, on the streets around me, in my friends' apartments, and on subways and buses. Babble, babble, babble, is what it sounded like—a din of voices and a sea of faces of different colors and shades of brown, white, yellow. It fascinated me, and still does. We never knew or thought about "legal" or "illegal." Most of my mother's friends spoke with accents of one kind or another; so did any of the various helpers she found over the years so she could go out to work, especially when my brother and I were very young. Peggy, who took care of me and gave me piggyback rides when I was a toddler, had an Irish lilt; she even took me to church with her on her days off, so I could dip my hand in the holy water, which was fun. Maureen, who gave me baths and dried me with a rough towel, had lovely red hair and another kind of almost-Irish voice; she sang. Georgia, who had dark black skin and made delicious fried chicken, smoked a corncob pipe in the kitchen of our apartment after supper. We didn't call them "flats;" they were apartments, no matter how small, no matter how few stories the buildings had. Sometimes we kids even called them our "houses," as in

"May I go over to Audrey's house to play?"

We were all, one way or another, children or grandchildren of immigrants.

No one that I knew then used that word. Nor had they ever heard "race" or "ethnicity." They said "nationality," as in my poem, "What *Are* You?" (p. 48) Were we bigoted? It depended on what we heard at home, and some heard enough that they freely used the parental "wop, kike, chink, spic"—but not all of them did.

I don't think I ever did myself.

As an adult in the 21st century of what is still, hopefully, the United States of America, I'm now exposed to ugly talk about immigrants and "illegals," even though most of the people who wait on us in restaurants, who come as home health aides to help us out, who work here on their college vacations at our tourist resorts, ski lifts and other such places are not from here. Many are on tourist visas; others just come, legally or not. All, however, have migrated.

Our local hospitals and medical centers have translators in multiple languages.

So the delicious babble, babble, babble that enchanted me as a child continues.

Yet there are those who think the only way we can become what we were meant to be as a country is to stifle it; stuff something into the mouth of all that babble and have it come out as English—or what passes for English among those who think this way.

The idea for this anthology came to me when my longtime friend, Jim Haba, sent his poem "Let Them Come" along with his 2019 New Year's message. It exploded with meaning, and the first words, "What they bring…" seemed perfect for a title. So, impulsively, and still on a high from the first (and I thought the last) anthology I had done, *Climate of Opinion: Sigmund Freud in Poetry* (IPBooks, 2017), I asked Jim if he would like to co-edit a new one. To my delight he said he would. So here we are now, on the edge of this exciting, important and increasingly timely new project. The last time around, I was fortunate enough to obtain funding that allowed me to pay myself and the publisher a little something and each of the poets a little something also. As a longtime writer and member of the Authors' Guild, I believe that content providers should always be paid. Unfortunately, most poets make hardly anything from their work—unless they "dumb it down" to a Hallmark level. If that makes me sound like an elitist, I have to confess to being something of a snob about poetry. I believe I know a good poem when I see it—and this time I have someone else—my good friend, Jim—to help anchor me. Like the last time, we have managed to obtain some funding, most of which will go for permissions, and much gratitude is due to the American Psychoanalytic Association for this.

And now, so soon this time after the last anthology, here are these poems to help you think about migration and immigration and to feel deeply and empathize, which is why this is a book of poems and not a treatise or thesis, not even a book of essays—although I must admit that some recent books of short essays, notably Ross Gay's marvelous *Book of Delights* (Algonquin Books of Chapel Hill, 2019), is as effective as a long lyric poem, such as Claudia Rankine's *Citizen: An American Lyric* (Graywolf, 2014), from which we have been given permission to use a section (p. 22) Uh-oh, there I go again, the old English teacher, recommending book after book. Please forgive.

–Irene Willis

Now that I've told you my version of how this book came to be, here is Jim himself telling you what he thinks about our project:

We are a nation of immigrants, since even the first Americans seem to have come from elsewhere, probably from Asia by way of a land bridge from Siberia to Alaska. Unlike all subsequent waves of immigration to this hemisphere, their arrival apparently did not threaten or in any way affect the existence of a resident human population. That potential threat posed by immigrants—which could be as fundamental as any difference beyond those regularly recognized and tolerated by a resident population—seems to be at the heart of the current sharply divided response to immigration around the world.

The commonly used term "waves of immigration" reminds us that immigration is, in fact, as natural and inevitable as the movement of water: brooks, streams, rivers and tides. An ancient Japanese motto even says "Live like water." That we instinctively link immigration with water reveals our understanding that, at some level, immigration is an essential feature of life (especially, but not only, human life) and that immigrants always bring something of fundamental value to the resident population.

So, beyond meeting the immediate need to protect and control their identity and assets, any resident population must also, for the sake of long-term health and development, learn how to accept and incorporate the new beliefs, qualities, foods and genes brought by immigrants.

In other words, from the beginning we have had to learn how to live with each other if we are to live at all. And the first step in achieving that goal may be in learning how to value each other. Learning, in short, what we need that these strange and different others, coming into and stirring up our lives, could be bringing to us.

To understand and absorb the profound questions inherent in immigration we need art, because art exists, like immigration itself, outside the ordinary parameters of experience. And of the arts, perhaps we need poems most, because of how they combine the elusive, imaginative nature of story with the historically charged and intimately familiar nature of words and metaphor.

We experience poems as immigrants: strange, even slightly wild infiltrators of our apparently secure and comfortable existence, their incursion always accompanied by the re-enlivening shock of the new.

–Jim Haba

Emma Lazarus   The New Colossus

Not like the brazen giant of Greek fame,
With conquering limbs astride from land to land;
Here at our sea-washed sunset gates shall stand
A mighty woman with a torch, whose flame
Is the imprisoned lightning, and her name
MOTHER OF EXILES. From her beacon-hand
Glows world-wide welcome; her mild eyes command
The air-bridged harbor that twin cities frame.

"Keep, ancient lands, your storied pomp!" cries she
with silent lips. "Give me your tired, your poor,
your huddled masses yearning to breathe free,
the wretched refuse of your teeming shore.
Send these, the homeless, tempest-tossed to me,
I lift my lamp beside the golden door!"

Pastor Martin Niemoller

First They Came

First they came for the Communists
And I did not speak out
Because I was not a Communist
Then they came for the Socialists
And I did not speak out
Because I was not a Socialist
Then they came for the trade unionists
And I did not speak out
Because I was not a trade unionist
Then they came for the Jews
And I did not speak out
Because I was not a Jew
Then they came for me
And there was no one left
To speak out for me.

Jim Haba   **Let Them Come**

What they bring is always more than

what we thought we needed. They carry it

in their bodies and in their dreams—

the enduring, the new, the unimaginable,

the beloved, the holy, the children

of our children's children's children.

These angels too

marvelous, holy, ecstatic,

determined, generous, enduring,

alien, penniless, vagrant,

unschooled, unsponsored, undocumented

immigrants among us.

Robert Frost

Mending Wall

Something there is that doesn't love a wall,
That sends the frozen-ground-swell under it,
And spills the upper boulders in the sun;
And makes gaps even two can pass abreast.
The work of hunters is another thing;
I have come after them and made repair
Where they have left not one stone on a stone,
But they would have the rabbit out of hiding,
To please the yelping dogs. The gaps I mean,
No one has seen them made or heard them made,
But at spring mending-time we find them there.
I let my neighbor know beyond the hill;
And on a day we meet to walk the line
And set the wall between us once again.
We keep the wall between us as we go.
To each the boulders that have fallen to each.
And some are loaves and some so nearly balls
We have to use a spell to make them balance:
"Stay where you are until our backs are turned!"
We wear our fingers rough with handling them.
Oh, just another kind of out-door game,
One on a side. It comes to little more;
There where it is we do not need the wall;
He is all pine and I am apple orchard.
My apple trees will never get across
And eat the cones under his pines. I tell him.

He only says, "Good fences make good neighbors."
Spring is the mischief in me, and I wonder
If I could put a notion in his head:
"*Why* do they make good neighbors? Isn't it
where there are cows. But here there are no cows.
Before I built a wall I'd ask to know
what I was walling in or walling out,
and to whom I was like to give offense.
Something there is that doesn't love a wall,
That wants it down." I could say "Elves" to him,
But it's not elves exactly, and I'd rather
He said it for himself. I see him there
Bringing a stone grasped firmly by the top
In each hand, like an old stone-savage armed.
He moves in darkness as it seems to me,
Not of wood only and the shade of trees.
He will not go behind his father's saying,
And he likes having thought of it so well
He says again, "Good fences make good neighbors."

Do you remember our earnestness, our sincerity
in first grade when we learned to sing "America

The Beautiful" along with the "Star-Spangled Banner"
and say the Pledge of Allegiance to America

We put our hands over our first grade hearts
we felt proud to be citizens of America

School days school days dear old Golden Rule Days
when we learned how to behave in America

What to wear, how to smoke, how to despise our parents
who didn't understand us or America

Only later learning the *Banner* and the *Beautiful*
live on opposite sides of the street in America

Only later discovering the Nation is divisible
by money by power by color by gender by sex America

We comprehend it now this land is two lands
one triumphant bully one still hopeful America

Imagining amber waves of grain blowing in the wind
purple mountains and no homeless in America

Sometimes I still put my hand tenderly on my heart
somehow or other still carried away by America

Alicia Ostriker   **Ghazal: America**

My grandfather's pipe tobacco fragrance, moss-green
   cardigan, his Yiddish lullaby
when I woke crying: three of my earliest memories in
   America

Arriving on time for the first big war, remaining for the
   second, sad grandpa
who walked across Europe to get to America

When the babies starved, when the village burned, when
   you were flogged
log out, ship out, there was a dream, the green breast of
   America

My grandfather said no president including Roosevelt
   would save the Jews in Europe
he drew out an ample handkerchief and wiped away the
   weeping of America

One thing that makes me happy about my country
is that Allen Ginsberg could fearlessly write the comic
   poem "America"

Route 66 entices me westward toward dreaming California
I adore superhighways but money is the route of all evil in
   America.

Let miners curse mines let workers curse bosses let
    football curse management
Let me curse the makers of bombs over Baghdad here in
    America

When I video your rivers your painterly meadows your
    public sculpture Rockies
when I walk in your crooked cities I love you so much I
    bless you so much America

People people look there: grandpa please look: Liberty
    the Shekhina herself
welcoming you like a queen, like a goddess, to America

Take the flute player from his mesa, take the raven from
    his tree
now that the buffalo is gone from America

White man, the blacks are snarling, the yellow swarming
    the umber terrorists
are tunneling through and breathing your air of fear in
    America

If you will it, it is no dream, somebody admonished my
    grandfather
he surmised they meant survival in America

Chris Fogg   Ladybirds

We're being overrun by ladybirds,
they creep through every crook and crevice,
flop on windowsill and work-top—
such exotic splash of colour
in these dark, damp grey days.

But it seems they're not welcome,
they're the wrong type—foreign interlopers,
voracious harlequin invaders,
marauding Ghengis Khan hordes
hammering the window panes.

There's no stopping them,
they resist all forms of pest control,
carried on the wind, washed up by the tide,
not tunnels, not fences can hold them back,
vampire swarm, they suck our native species dry.
Like bluebells—

The English flower too's become diluted,
in danger of extinction, a last century relic,
but *ancient regime* in breeding can't avert
their Tsars' doomed haemophilia.

Diversity brings strength—
the air teems with new arrivals' thrumming
wing beats, I open windows wide,
look out towards the woods where next spring
clouds of paint-box blues will carpet the paths.

A ladybird alights on my finger—
let them all come, I say.

al-Maarri asks, which rings true, which shout can be
   heard loudest?
My students are five, and I tell them we need to get ready
   to help

our Syrian on Monday. They know who speaks Arabic, as
they know
their own homeland, Bengali, Vietnamese, Spanish,
   Chinese, Gujarati, Hebrew,

and now a story they do not know. No amount
of bears in the
woods can keep them from telling me what they will
   bring to school,

their toys, clothes and trinkets. A cardinal is on the barest
   of trees
searching for the frozen berries on this bitter day, and no
   amount

of beak to limb can loosen the fruit. Where is he, caught
   in his high tower?
What would he twitter if he saw us waiting at the door?

Ted Kooser   **At Nightfall**

In feathers the color of dusk, a swallow,
up under the shadowy eaves of the barn,
weaves now, with skillful beak and chitter,
one bright white feather into her nest
to guide her flight home in the darkness.
It has taken a hundred thousand years
for a bird to learn this one trick with a feather,
a simple thing. And the world is alive
with such innocent progress. But to what
safe place shall any of us return
in the last smoky nightfall,
when we in our madness have put the torch
to the hope in every nest and feather?

James Kelleher   **I Worry How I Appear Before God**

I never worked or risked enough.
Stubborn son of calloused immigrants,
contrite for lost years dreamed away,
I stretched my youth in play.

Old, I return your smooth sea stones,
arching green pines, red sunsets;
your iridescent purple humming birds,
hooting owls, moose, mice, mist rising
on the Margaree River; and your sun,
luminous on clear ocean salt water.

I return these wonders you let me see
in the simple poems I write and say.

Lori Desrosiers   Ashkenazy

My mother used to say to me,
Don't tell people you're Jewish.

Fear of others in the shadows,
of extermination, of being taken,
everything taken.

We danced the Horah at weddings.
Twice a year we went to Temple;
Rosh Hashanah to hear the cantors

on Yom Kippur
the Kol Nidre's mournful song.

My people are removed from the ancestors
scattered from Odessa to Philadelphia to California.

Before that—
we forget.

Our tongues echo
a smattering of Yiddish,
a few Russian words.

The voice of the great grandfather
who was a cantor,
whose name we don't know,

rings in my brother's baritone;
the same voice as our grandfather,
who had no time to sing.

W.H. Auden

Refugee Blues

Say this city has ten million souls
Some are living in mansions, some are living in holes:
Yet there's no place for us, my dear, yet there's no place
    for us.

Once we had a country and we thought it fair,
Look in the atlas and you'll find it there:
We cannot go there now, my dear, we cannot go there
    now.

In the village churchyard there grows an old yew,
Every spring it blossoms anew:
Old passports can't do that, my dear, old passports can't do
    that.

The consul banged the table and said,
"If you've got no passport, you're officially dead":
But we are still alive, my dear, but we are still alive.

Went to a committee; they offered me a chair;
Asked me politely to return next year:
But where shall we go today, my dear, but where shall we
    go today?

Came to a public meeting; the speaker got up and said;
"If we let them in, they will steal our daily bread";
He was talking of you and me, my dear, he was talking of
   you and me.

Thought I heard the thunder rumbling in the sky:
It was Hitler over Europe, saying, "They must die";
O we were in his mind, my dear, O we were in his mind.

Saw a poodle in a jacket fastened with a pin,
Saw a door opened and a cat let in:
But they weren't German Jews, my dear, but they weren't
   German Jews.

Went down in a harbour and stood upon the quay,
Saw the fish swimming as if they were free:
Only ten feet away, my dear, only ten feet away.

Walked through a wood, saw birds in the trees;
They had no politicians and sang at their ease:
They weren't the human race, my dear, they weren't the
   human race.

Dreamed I saw a building with a thousand floors,
A thousand windows and a thousand doors:
Not one of them was ours, my dear, not one of them was
    ours.

Stood on a great plain in the falling snow;
Ten thousand soldiers marched to and fro:
Looking for you and me, my dear, looking for you and me.

Tracy K. Smith   The United States Welcomes You

Why and by whose power were you sent?

What do you see that you may wish to steal?

Why this dancing? Why do your dark bodies

Drink up all the light? What are you demanding

That we feel? Have you stolen something? Then

What is that leaping in your chest? What is

The nature of your mission? Do you seek

To offer a confession? Have you anything to do

With others brought by us to harm? Then

Why are you afraid? And why do you invade

Our night, hands raised, eyes wide, mute

As ghosts? Is there something you wish to confess?

Is this some enigmatic type of test? What if we

Fail? How and to whom do we address our appeal?

Claudia Rankine   **The New Therapist**

The new therapist specializes in trauma counseling. You
have only ever spoken on the phone. Her house has
a side gate that leads to a back entrance she uses for
patients. You walk down a path bordered on both sides
with deer grass and rosemary to the gate, which turns out
to be locked.

At the front door the bell is a small round disc that you
press firmly. When the door finally opens, the woman
standing there yells, at the top of her lungs, Get away
from my house! What are you doing in my yard?

It's as if a wounded Doberman pinscher or a German
shepherd has gained the power of speech. And though
you back up a few steps, you manage to tell her you have
an appointment. You have an appointment? she spits
back. Then she pauses. Everything pauses. Oh, she says,
followed by, oh, yes, that's right. I am sorry.

I am so sorry, so, so sorry.

Father Tongue

Before I left him,
my Greek father,
I asked
for his watch.

I'd always admired
its steely measuring face,
stainless and all-American

I tore off to France,
wore it like him
on my thin wrist,

liked to feel
its heft

this sliver of armor,
anchor from home.

I'd eyed
his vintage
Webster's, too,

this book,
my traveling companion

purloined glossary
from between the wars

O father, Odysseus of the field,
post office, shoe factory, and Ray-
theon Corporation

Why do I take your journey
in re-
verse,

homeward bound

not from Greece
but from Massachusetts?

How the tome and the time
feel so stolid in my hand—

what I thought was our inheritance—

I am in its prise,
not the other way around.

In Paris
I had a dream—

human mirage
hovering

just out of reach

Father and mother
reunited
in miniature oval

both
daguerreotype and *ikona*

A mirror-river
trembled slightly

before emptying from my eyes.

Anne Porter

Susanna

Nobody in the hospital
Could tell the age
Of the old woman who
was called Susanna

I knew she spoke some English
and that she was an immigrant
Out of a little country
Trampled by armies

Because she had no visitors
I would stop by to see her
But she was always sleeping

All I could do
Was to get out her comb
And carefully untangle
The tangles in her hair

One day I was beside her
When she woke up
Opening small dark eyes
Of a surprising clearness

She looked at me and said
You want to know the truth?
I answered Yes

She said it's something that
My mother told me

There's not a single inch
Of our whole body
That the Lord does not love

Alberto Rios   A House Called Tomorrow

1952

You are not fifteen, or twelve, or seventeen—
You are a hundred wild centuries

And fifteen, bringing with you
In every breath and in every step

Everyone who has come before you
All the yous that you have been,

The mothers of your mother,
The fathers of your father.

If someone in your family tree was trouble,
A hundred were not:

The bad do not win—not finally,
No matter how loud they are.

We simply would not be here
If that were so.

You are made, fundamentally, from the good.
With this knowledge, you never march alone.

You are the breaking news of the century.
You are the good who has come forward

Through it all, even if so many days
Feel otherwise. But think:

When you as a child learned to speak,
It's not that you didn't know words—

It's that, from the centuries, you knew so many,
And it's hard to choose the words that will be your own.

From those centuries we human beings bring with us
The simple solutions and songs,

The river bridges and star charts and song harmonies
All in service to a simple idea:

That we can make a house called tomorrow.
What we bring, finally, into the new day, every day,

Is ourselves. And that's all we need
to start. That's everything we require to keep going.

Look back only for as long as you must,
Then go forward into the history you will make.

Be good, then better. Write books. Cure disease.
Make us proud. Make yourself proud.

And those who came before you? When you hear thunder,
Hear it as their applause.

Irene Willis   **Border**

"A 'Heartbreaking' Scene at the Border:
A Toddler Found Wandering Alone"
—*NY Times,* April 25, 2019

If reporters have their
hearts broken
can yours be broken too,

poor reader, trying to eat your
breakfast while that 3-year-old
has none—

your fingers smudged from
newsprint when the toddler's
are filled with grit?

Questions for the soul or intellect—
where to begin as we gulp our coffee
scarf down toast

carefully reach for vitamins to swallow
with water fresh from the tap
supplements for God-given nutrients

sustenance, abundance, wealth.

Lavinia Kumar   **Refugees Near Calais, France**

They've come to find peace and work,
but are stopped in Calais, hope for a ride
to take them north under the Channel.

They sleep cold in tents, in parking lots
controlled by Afghans, who push away
those skin-dark—Ifa, Heeran, Rashad,

from Ethiopia, Sudan, Eritria, shot
sometimes robbed—one left naked—
clothes, shoes, phone taken.

He walked the long road back to camp,
joined a winding line for food bowl.
He is always hungry, dreams an end

to enduring. Now only wants to jump
into a moving truck, hide from driver
and customs, hold on. Live again.

W.S. Merwin   Emigré

You will find it is
much as you imagined
in some respects
which no one can predict
you will be homesick
at times for something you can describe
and at times without being able to say
what you miss
just as you used to feel when you were at home

some will complain from the start
that you club together
with your own kind
but only those who have
done what you have done
conceived of it longed for it
and have come out with
no money no papers nothing
at your age knowing what you have done
what you are talking about
and will find you a roof and employers

others will say from the start
that you avoid
those of your country
for a while
as your country becomes
a category in the new place
and nobody remembers the same things
in the same way
and you come to the problem
of what to remember after all
and of what is your real
language

where does it come from what does it
sound like
who speaks it

if you cling to the old usage
do you not cut yourself off
from the new speech
but if you rush to the new lips
do you not fade like a sound cut off
do you not dry up like a puddle
is the new tongue to be trusted

what of the relics of your childhood
should you bear in mind pieces
of dyed cotton and gnawed wood
lint of voices untranslatable stories
summer sunlight on dried paint
whose color continues to fade in the
growing brightness of the white afternoon
ferns on the shore of the transparent lake
or should you forget them
as you float between ageless languages
and call from one to the other who you are

Ted Kooser   **The Great-Grandparents**

As small children, we were taken to meet them.
They had recently arrived from another world
and stood dumbfounded in the busy depot
of the present, their useless belongings in piles:
old tools, old words, old recipes, secrets.
They searched our faces and grasped our hands
as if we could lead them back, but we drew them
forward into the future, feeling them tremble,
their shirt cuffs yellow, smoky old woodstoves
smoldering somewhere under their clothes.

This is the first night in our house. This is our house, this
    first night.
How the traffic lights change colors. Colors change like
    bomb shells.

Shells we can find at the beach, we can sleep, each one on
    our own bed—
we cannot sleep alone, each room its own sadness, the
    quiet of the streets.

The curtains we do not have, the sheets to cover the
    windows, the sheets
we never had in the camps, the house is ours, and we
    cannot trust it.

The children run their hands on the bathroom tiles, turn
    the water on and off,
just to see it pour freely. Tomorrow they will go to school
on a yellow bus.

How do I know when they return, when even the clocks
    have numbers in a language
I cannot understand? The sink drips and we are afraid to
    get out of bed, each drop

a tear, each plink a breath I am not ready to breathe.

Martín Espada　　　　　　　　　　　　　　　　　　**Bully**

Boston, Massachusetts, 1987

In the school auditorium,
the Theodore Roosevelt statue
is nostalgic
for the Spanish-American War,
each fist lonely for a saber
or the reins of anguish-eyed horses,
or a podium to clatter with speeches
glorying in the malaria of conquest.

But now the Roosevelt school
is pronounced *Hernandez.*
Puerto Rico has invaded Roosevelt
with its army of Spanish-speaking children
in the hallways,
brown children devouring
the stockpile of the cafeteria,
children painting Taino ancestors
who leap naked across murals.

Roosevelt is surrounded
by all the faces
he ever shoved in eugenic spite
and cursed as mongrels, skin of one race,
hair and cheekbones of another.

Once Marines tramped
from the newsreel of his imagination;
now children plot to spray graffiti
in parrot-brilliant colors
across the Victorian mustache
and monocle.

Michael Waters

I don't want anyone to explain
this bicycle brought across the ocean.
The streets of the new world
are paved, if lucky,

by husbands who surrender trade
to the steam of tar, who
labor with such precise sorrow
their sons soon leave home.

Photographs become precious:
how proud she looks beside her bicycle!
And in her eyes, here,
that particular shade of green

must still burn
to bargain marriage, cross
borders toward the year of my birth.
One family

breeds the immigration
officials, the next
reasons for fleeing continents—
I don't want anyone to explain.

Anyway you try to make sense
of the past...sighs my father,
shuffling photographs,
revising the pale histories...

but this bicycle blazes in sunlight!

Moja Kahf — My Grandmother Washes Her Feet In the Bathroom at Sears

My grandmother puts her feet in the sink
   of the bathroom at Sears
to wash them in the ritual washing for prayer,
   wudu,
because she has to pray in the store or miss
the mandatory prayer for Muslims
She does it with great poise, balancing
herself with one plump matronly arm
against the automated hot-air hand dryer,
after having removed her support knee-highs
and laid them aside, folded in thirds,
and given me her purse and her packages to hold
so she can accomplish this august ritual
and get back to the ritual of shopping for housewares

Respectable Sears matrons shake their heads and frown
as they notice what my grandmother is doing,
an affront to American porcelain,
a contamination of American Standards
by something foreign and unhygienic
requiring civic action and possible use of disinfectant spray
They fluster about and flutter their hands and I can see
a clash of civilizations brewing in the Sears bathroom.

My grandmother, though she speaks no English,
catches their meaning and her look in the mirror says,
I have washed my feet over Iznik tile in Istanbul
with water from the world's ancient irrigation systems
I have washed my feet in the bathhouses of Damascus
over painted bowls imported from China
among the best families of Aleppo
and if you Americans knew anything
about civilization and cleanliness,
you'd make wider washbins, anyway.
My grandmother knows one culture—the right one,

as do these matrons of the Middle West. For them,
my grandmother might as well have been squatting in the
    mud
over a rusty tin in vaguely tropical squalor,
Mexican or Middle Eastern, it doesn't matter which,
when she lifts her well-groomed foot and puts it over the
    edge.
"You can't do that," one of the women protests,
turning to me. "Tell her she can't do that."
"We wash our feet five times a day,"
my grandmother declares hotly in Arabic.
"My feet are cleaner than their sink.
Worried about their sink, are they? I
should worry about my feet!"
My grandmother nudges me, "Go on, tell them."

Standing between the door and the mirror, I can see
at multiple angles, my grandmother and the other
    shoppers,
all of them decent and goodhearted women, diligent
in cleanliness, grooming and decorum.
Even now, my grandmother, not to be rushed,
is delicately drying her pumps with tissues from her purse
For my grandmother always wears well-turned pumps
That match her purse, I think in case someone
from one of the best families of Aleppo
should run into her—here, in front of the Kenmore display.
I smile at the midwestern women
as if my grandmother has just said something lovely about
    them
and shrug at my grandmother as if they
had just apologized through me.
No one is fooled but I

hold the door open for everyone
and we all emerge on the sales floor
and lose ourselves in the great common ground
of housewares on markdown.

Hilda Weisert

The Transit Hall on Pier 86

They say there's a place in the brain for faces
and I believe it, this headache a claw
into raw nerves, the strain of testing
so many men's faces for my one "Father"

as the boat empties and the transit hall
fills with women, children, and one plausible man
after another whose face dissolves
with study. For a moment each one

could be him, ruddy, regular, a gaze returned
into my face, which has its own brain
place also working hard to make
something recognizable as a daughter

out of so many raw nerves. The looking and the looked-at
swim—these places in the brain are wet, gelid,
something out of Coelenterata that starts to wave
at this handsome new father until his hard

square eyes break my floundering smile
into one more mistake. A decade is long
when you are twenty. The long hall rings
with "Hellos!", feet on pavement, the clamoring

embrace. When I see him, I am alone,
and at his eyes, drop my own, ashamed
I tried so many strangers on, itinerants against
the one face that goes here, and whose eyes

I could have lost when they are the same
as mine. Mine that I work to raise, bringing up
a woman's face out of a child's, and offering my father
a hand, dry and outstretched.

Suzanne Gardinier

Refugees

Every night she dreams of departure
from successive islands of suffering
There is no mainland There is no knowing
The depth of any one island's pain
until after her feet have settled on
the new and she looks back over the water
but the glare blinds and her eyes are tired
and already she can't remember
On each new island are the orders
in the barked opaque new words A nod
means No A wave means Go Away A pointed
finger means here is the dirty place
for you to wait to clean to sleep to live
Each island has its ordure to be removed
food to be cooked children to be tended
and saves these tasks for its most recent
strangers its little-loved On her knees
on the floor or over the steaming heap
of clothes that are not hers by the crib
of the baby who is not here and will
not stop crying a sudden sweep of her hand
reminds her of a gesture from the last
island but it is gone in a minute
The one she stands on she calls This new world
The one she has left forgotten she calls Home

Irene Willis   **What Are You?**

What *are* you?
Was the first question
the kids in my new neighborhood—
in every one of my new neighborhoods—
would ask, right after, What's your name?

The first time, I didn't know
what they meant. I was eight
and new at this.

A person, I'd say. A human being.
A girl. What do you *think* I am?
You know what we mean, they'd say.
What nationality?

American, I'd say. I'm American.

They'd laugh. You can't be.
Nobody is. You have to be
something.

Irene Willis — The Secret at the Back of the Cupboard

New York City, 1939

*The thing you are most afraid to write,
write that.*

—*Nayyirah Waheed*

Why wouldn't it be better to hide
inside my mother's secret?

Why wouldn't it be better to stay with her
in the box at the back of the cupboard

with the matzoh and the kosher salt,
away from the cleaning woman's

and the janitor's scorn?

Why wouldn't it be better not to see that
look on their faces and the turning away?

I read once of a Christmas tree hung
with images of dead Jews

in a German living-room.

In those days we were hiding from
Vannie, our German housekeeper

in New York.

Later we hid from my mother's
Irish second husband.

Don't tell anyone, my mother said
of the secret place she led me to.

Don't ever tell, she said, breaking
a piece of matzoh and dipping it

into her saccharin-laced coffee.

As she sipped and stirred, I listened.
Eight years old, nine, thirteen

and later still.

I can tell what you are, said the woman
I beat out of a parking space

in a crowded suburban lot
just by looking at you.

I was so afraid, so sure I knew what she meant
that I didn't have the guts to ask.

I should have said, *What? What am I?*
to hear her say whatever, but I couldn't.

Better to stay in the box in the cupboard
with my mother's secret.

And now her ashes, heavier than I knew,
with their bits of bone, in a box

at the back of my closet.

Julia Alvarez   Spic

U.S.A., 1960

Out in the playground, kids were shouting *Spic!*
Lifting my sister's skirt, yanking her slip.
Younger, less sexy, I was held and stripped
of coat and bookbag. Homework tumbled out
onto oncoming traffic on the street.
Irregular verbs crumpled under trees
of frantic taxis, blew against the grates
of uptown buses we would later take
when school let out, trailed by cries of *Spic!*
What did they want, these American kids?

That night when we asked Mami, she explained:
our classmates had been asking us to *speak,*
not to be so unfriendly, running off
without a word. "This is Amèrica!
The anthem here invites its citizens
to speak up. *Oh see, can you say,*" she sang,
proving her point, making us sing along.
She winked at Papi, who had not joined in
but bowed his head, speaking instead to God
to protect his daughters in America.

I took her at her word: I raised my hand,
speaking up during classes, recess time.
The boys got meaner. *Spic ball!* they called out,
tossing off my school beanie, playing catch
while I ran boy to boy to get it back.
They sacked my stolen lunch box for their snacks,
dumping the foreign things in the garbage bin,
Spic trash! But I kept talking, telling them
how someday when I'd learn their language well,
I'd say what I'd seen in America.

One what?—
Nigger, kike, wop, honky, paddy, redneck, frog,
cocksucker, bastard, bitch, motherfucker, dog-
punk, nerd, dweeb, sissy, jerkoff, creep,
queen, faggot, bulldyke, Republican sheep,
right-wing, leftist, Trotskyite, capitalist pig,
facelifted faketitted phony-in-a-wig,
impotent, premature ejaculator,
stand-up comic, poet, actor,
waiter, chauffeur, screenwriter, masturbator,
codependent, alcoholic, addict, abuser,
liar, cheater, thief, quitter, loser,
photographer, reporter, lawyer, dealer,
doctor, chef, model, hair-stylist, healer,
quack, booshie, commie, jock, gambler, gangster,
fuck-up, greedhead, homie, rambler, prankster,
hippie, yuppie, beatnik, artist, freak,
monster, asskisser, cartoonist, geek,
hoser, dickhead, wanker, slant-eyes dwarf,
fatso, pasty-face, nothing-but-soft,
sexist, racist, ageist, whore,
Buddhist, born-again, sober bore,
white, brown, yellow, red, black and blue,
he, she, them, us, it, me, you,
rocks, mountains, clouds, trees,
rivers, valleys, inlets, seas,
birds, horses, whales, kittens, bees …

Hey!—
This could go on forever,
when all we really gotta say is:
Everything and us—

Us

        and

              everything—

from the smallest quark
to the biggest galaxy—
it's all the same,
and it only takes one
to know one.

One what?

Cynthia Read Gardner   Haiti After the Flood

The women wade across a water plain

holding children's hands.

No clear destination,

no shore.

Atop their heads

bundles

wrapped in cloth:

clouds

newly gathered.

Martín Espada — Jorge the Church Janitor Finally Quits

Cambridge, Massachusetts, 1989

No one asks
where I am from,
I must be
from the country of janitors,
I have always mopped this floor.
Honduras, you are a squatter's camp
outside the city
of their understanding.

No one can speak
my name,
I host the fiesta
of the bathroom,
stirring the toilet
like a punchbowl.
The Spanish music of my name
is lost
when the guests complain
about toilet paper.

What they say
must be true:
I am smart
but I have a bad attitude.

No one knows
that I quit tonight,
maybe the mop
will push on without me,
sniffing along the floor
like a crazy squid
with stringy gray tentacles.
They will call it Jorge.

The upper flat on Salem Avenue, the red and gray
linoleum of the kitchen floor, the cold bathroom and coral
Lifebuoy soap, the deafening sounds of the motorcycles
being repaired in the backyard by the man who lived
downstairs. I remember that back yard—it had no grass.
Not one shred of green.

My grandfather bringing dozens of small chicks into the
house for me to see, the soft yellow of their down, their
scurrying all over the kitchen floor, pooping all over the
place. I remember my mother yelling, my grandfather's
brown teeth laughing.

Union School off Broadway—all the immigrant children
in my kindergarten class drawing pictures of cats, dogs,
cows, horses. I remember the girl from the Urals
with the red ribbon in her hair who drew her black cat in
silence, who never spoke.

The dull maroon uniforms the girls had to wear at
St. Wenceslas Elementary School in a gray suburb of
Cleveland. I remember by February of every year, the
backs of the skirts would be threadbare and worn from our
constant sitting, sitting in our cramped desks.

Sister Bertha and the wart on her tongue; Sister Brendan's breaking a yardstick over Glenn Tokas' head. I remember Sister Concepta Marie's lovely ankles covered in black.

West Virginia and the visit to my mother's cousin, Sister Matilda the Carmelite. I remember the steel mills of Weirton and their huge smoke stacks: how they made the sky nothing but orange—sky, clouds, air.

My fourth-grade class in the basement. Room 1. I couldn't get any more subterranean than that. Jerome Polonsky opening a window to let a cat in the room who slinked its way from the basement window well to the top of the room's storage cabinet, sat there, and peed. I remember Sister Brendan's face getting red, redder, her making Jerome crawl up to get the cat. "Clean that mess up!!!"

Being scared to death of my mother's old aunt. Streena, the woman with no voice, who could only breathe out strange Polish words through a tiny hole in her neck. *Nie, nie. Gdzie zob moja corka*, she'd impatiently rasp. I remember sitting in her dark living room surrounded by icons of the Black Madonna.

Being lost in the great expanse of ragweeds, Queen Anne's lace, junipers, maples and pines that created my Uncle Stanley's huge backyard. He grew hybrid orchids in his small greenhouse attached to the garage. Their petals heavy with white, fuchsia, yellow. He also raised exotic fish in endless rows of tanks in his basement. I remember still being lost as I slowly walked the labyrinth of walls of water, the aquarium's glow.

Losing my favorite doll: a dark-haired ballerina in pink tights and frilly tutu. She had a porcelain face, deep brown eyes, legs and arms that could move and bend. One day I awoke and couldn't find her anywhere. I remember thinking she just got tired of living in my house and decided to leave, to walk away and never come back.

A dream I had before I could talk. I was in a huge forest
and the branches of the trees were like broken arms, the
sunlight throwing their shadows on the forest floor where
I stood still and alone. I saw nothing but the green air of
the trees. I heard nothing but the low moan of the wind.
Finally, from the edge of the woods came a soft sound. It
was the voice of my grandmother: my mother's mother,
the one who died before I was born. She was singing in
a language that even the trees could understand. She was
singing and calling my name. I remember I
awoke and spoke my first word. *Matka.*

We walk down this street of aromas, knowing
glasses of water left on the restaurant table
will shake in the hands of the waitress
carrying them off.
                              As she spoke to our table
the tat of an angel on her arm
was also speaking a language we started
to learn. Arabic?
                              She spoke of prayer
and asylum as equally inscrutable, broken
between two languages; that sorrow is long;
that laughter only covers short
distances. As between tables,
as between bombs.
                              Her left ear remained
open for orders of food and drink. The ruptured
drum of the other, she said, still
shivers in her dreams of exploding
children. One of them
inked on her arm.

Marie Howe

Sixth Grade

Sixth Grade

The afternoon the neighborhood boys tied me and Mary
    Lou Mather
To Donny Ralph's father's garage doors, spread-eagled,
it was the summer they chased us almost every day.

Careening across the lawns they'd mowed for money,
on bikes they threw down, they'd catch us, lie on top of us,
then get up and walk away.

That afternoon Donny's mother wasn't home.
His nine sisters and brothers gone—even Gramps, who
    lived with them,
gone somewhere—the backyard empty, the big house quiet.

A gang of boys. They pulled the heavy garage doors down
and tied us to them with clothesline,
and Donny got the deer's leg severed from the buck his
    dad had killed

the year before, dried up and still fur-covered, and sort of
poked it at us, dancing around the blacktop in his
    sneakers, laughing.
Then somebody took it from Donny and did it.

And then somebody else, and somebody after him.
And then Donny pulled up Mary Lou's dress and held it up,
   and she began to cry, and I became a boy again
   and shouted Stop

and they wouldn't
And then a girl-boy calling out to Charlie, my best friend's
   brother,
who wouldn't look

Charlie! To my brother's friend who knew me
Stop them. And he wouldn't.
And then more softly, and looking directly at him, I said,
   Charlie.

And he said Stop. And they said What? And he said Stop it.
And they did, quickly untying the ropes, weirdly quiet,
Mary Lou still weeping. And Charlie? Already gone.

Charlotte Gould Warren   ## A Girl Tying Ribbons in Her Hair

—Immigrants

When I'm flying apart,
when my heart breaks,
when I feel too fractured

ever to mend, I walk out
into the afternoon, consider
the old boulder

scrubbed bare,
an erratic
the glacier left behind.

Soft rain from the over-hanging fir
mixes time and needles into
lichen's patient arrival.

Wrapping a wool scarf around my neck,
I run my hands along the tall stems
of winter grass.

How easily I'm hurt!—Even at my age
these chance collisions
call out the wounded child.

I want you to listen to me—
not with a lecture or silence—
with an echoing heart.

Spring water deepens in the bay.
Like Hindu dancers, coots pump their heads,
glide seamlessly.

A goat's head is bony,
a horse's muzzle inquisitive and warm—
these correspondences.

As a child, you learned to keep your pain buried,
to soldier on. I washed mine in tears, poems,
the language of marsh wrens.

We shelter each other, or
drift apart. Who could imagine
a granite boulder carried this far?

Or an iris on its tall stem
like a girl tying ribbons
in her hair?

Charlotte Gould Warren

Walking to School

Boarding School, Pennsylvania, 1947–53

I didn't have a bike them, but walked the few blocks
to Lower School, the only boarder that young.
Maple leaves scuffed into dancing, knee-deep
in the crackle and lightness, the pungent smell
coaxed into life again, my own brown leather shoes
double-knotted, laced with instruction. American,
fair-haired—looking like I belonged—I was new to the
    country,
born in India, daughter of missionaries, sure I was guilty
and innocent, letting my school books slip into the
    sheltering
leaves, the English sparrows chirping in a banter of
    shrubbery,
bright-beaked, fierce-eyed, flying me into the farthest
    branches.

Chris Waters

Field Notes

A man crosses a wide field
beneath an open sky

he leaves early with little luggage
putting darkness behind him

there is frost or dew or birdsong
he makes footprints in the new grass

that begin to look like tracks
if he hears a melody

he will stop then follow it
perhaps it is in the back of his head

maybe he hears it on the wind

but he follows it through the wide field

Detained

The sound of your own name
you soon forget, the river, its color
and depth. Without you, my other,
my heart is scarred by its beatings,
by the inheritance of silence
I've known my whole life
the barbed wire
behind which I was born, a drifting snow,
and the closing of the borders
our fathers crossed
and crossed back with stories of stars.
Our fathers, those temples of echoes.
Here, we burrow into the dark bars of our own hands.
In the red mud of the earth,
we are stripped and spat upon
and visited by fists and kicked,
and made to kneel we receive
the cold metal pipe in our anuses.
And while waiting to be released from this
we climb into the high beds of our mothers
where the world is more open,
is a sink of warm water,
is a ladle—someone is bathing us,
and combing our hair.

Then the tree in the prison yard
reaches over the wall,
picks the lock on the gate
and just like that, with nothing,
we are freed.

Marilyn Nelson   Minor Miracle

Which reminds me of another knock-on-wood
memory. I was cycling with a male friend,
through a small Midwestern town. We came to a 4-way
stop, and stopped, chatting. As we started again,
a rusty old pick-up truck, ignoring the stop sign,
hurricaned past scant inches from our front wheels.
My partner called, "Hey, that was a 4-way stop!"
The truck driver, stringy blond hair a long fringe
under his brand-name beer cap, looked back and yelled,
          "You fucking niggers!"

And sped off.
My friend and I looked at each other and shook our heads.
We remounted our bikes and headed out of town.
We were pedaling through a clear blue afternoon
between two fields of almost-ripened wheat
bordered by cornflowers and Queen Anne's lace
when we heard an unmuffled motor, a honk-honking.
We stopped, closed ranks, made fists.
It was the same truck. It pulled over.
A tall, very much in shape young white guy slid out:
greasy jeans, homemade finger tattoos, probably
a Marine Corps boot-camp footlockerfull
of martial arts techniques.

"What did you say back there!" he shouted.
My friend said "I said it was a 4-way stop.
You went through it."
"And what did I say?" the white guy asked.
"You said: You fucking niggers."
The afternoon froze.

"Well," said the white guy,
shoving his hands into his pockets
and pushing dirt around with the pointed toe of his boot,
"I just wanted to say I'm sorry."
He climbed back into his truck
and drove away.

Like old gods, some of us, far—
seeing. Ruined streets, plumes
of smoke over Ramadi, Sinjar,
flicker on our PC streams
from Syria or Myanmar.
Here, in Bodrum, Turkey, the still,
drowned body of a toddler;
there, wanderers through rubble.
Moving at dusk along a hill
toward Dobova with its poor
those more wretched, hopeful.

Our flesh pierced by rowel
to draw away the spreading germ,
we, too, take up the ritual
of living things—cold or warm,
carrying our sacks of bone-meal,
our prayers against harm.
The traveler's life is dual,
now airborne, now on land or reef.
We're scrappy as the ruff,
and trail past like the koel
his feathers; at times sleeping rough.

Leaving home's the first step,
and, most trying, the last;
x-marked on the heart's map
means leaving a past,
route of escape
through sand storm or snow-broth,
across flickering landscape,
slipping northward or south
your winding path
through ghetto or landslip
observing its Sabbaths.

Places must be left:
A keepsake watch
is the usual gift
to graduates, with a catch—
the bride at your wrist
now takes your pulse
and that exotic land
with its visa for ecstasy
is left behind
for a different country,
flatter, more bland.

Yet for some, there's the surprise
of winter landscape, an awe
kindled as Decembers arrive
with tapestries of snow
hung from trees by the river.
In storm you'll find a traveler's aid.
Ague that has its origins
in advancing age weighs
a little in later days,
the way snow quiets the engines
that would grind on flurried roads.

The mind turns counter-clock.
Yours drifts there every day,
floating in a leaky bark,
while body continues its way,
hands and feet and heart at work.
Events as templates—an olive
in the beak of the dove—recur:
Years pass; you fall in and out of
jobs, love. Now but to live
here and master the words
of an ark, tongue and groove.

A woman turns away her face.
With child, setting out to live
in another place, she will cross
city streets, fields, a grove.
A wheel rim lies flat on the grass,
where loamy soil marks a grave.
Sometimes a flying creature,
aloft, we leave home behind
for a country our own.
Crossing beyond border,
my feet clap a tune on wet sand.

You've felt your soul rise—who hasn't"—
coming to a new land; you've seen
below the moving continent;
smelled the rain-soaked earth, green
and pungent after the desert,
the far carapace of home,
and fallen to the charm
of some new chartered town,
Adams or Tyringham,
banded by field, by broken stone.

Some stones there are
that stand in rows in mown grass,
by now their chisel marks faint scars;
you'd settle here if ashes
weren't the thing for travelers:
like tiny moths they'll disperse,
drifting out; matter endures
but in some other spot
only the illusions cease.
(Bone takes a little longer:
so keep the fire hot.)

Sharon Olds

Secondary Boycott Ode

I had never seen anything like it. I was walking
out of the office of the braces doctor,
in the same building as the acne doctor,
I was on my way to the lunch counter
that had sandwiches on soft bread
with the crusts cut off—& people were blocking
the doors, following each other around
in a circle, like our junior high marching band,
& they were in the way, between me
& my sandwich. I went up to a lady who was watching,
& asked her what was happening,
& she told me about the segregated
lunch counters in the South—this was
a secondary boycott, of Woolworth's. & I asked,
how do they choose who walks, & she said,
Anyone can. I had never seen anyone
saying no with their body, with their feet.
When I stepped toward the circle, a man walked a little
faster, & a woman walked a little slower,
& there was a space for me, to sing
without making a sound, at last to be
unfaithful to my family,
stepping out on silence.

Kathleen Kraft   Swedish Fish

New York City, 1980

It was at Sweet Temptation on Madison Avenue
as I dropped Swedish Fish one at a time
into a small paper bag, when my friend Danni turned
to me and said, *You're a kike.*

I looked up surprised, stung, not by the word
but that it meant she might not like me.
I felt dirty and small and poor, though I was
none of those things. I stared back

at her eyes that looked like blue crystallized snowflakes,
saw my scattered reflection in them.
You don't know what you're talking about.
She smirked. We were 9 or 10, wearing our uniforms—

navy pinstripe jumpers over white button-down shirts.
That gift box of a store merged with her now
in all its perfect rows, the strands of confection—
Her hair was the longest and the blondest, a shining
mystery.

I went home with my bag of sweets and told my mother.
She probably heard it at home. She knew the family
but not well. Her father was involved
in the McCarthy hearings, on the wrong side.

Something about her mother being ill. She called them,
and Danni didn't call me any names after that. We had no
    more
play dates, which was fine because her apartment
was always dark and her mother loomed sadly.

Danni left the school eventually, and then I did.
There's no real record of her after that. No Aha searches
or social media pages to round out the story—
Just those red fish I still pick up to take home

to my mother, who has forgotten a lot—but we still love
    to chew them,
and they still get stuck in our teeth.

Erica Jong   Child on the Beach

The Mediterranean is black with bodies
as in the time of the Trojan War
when Homer sang of bloody battles
& heroes lay unburied
beneath the topless towers of Troy.

But this little boy of three
sleeps unburied on a beach.
Where is he from?
The chemical fog of Syria?
The garbage dumps of beautiful Beirut?
The chaos of civilization come undone?

He rests,
his parents lost,
his sisters drowned,
his brother thrown up on another beach…

What shall I do
with this dead toddler
who breaks me open to grief?

I will adopt him,
my nameless grandson,
welcome him into my shattered breast,
his death so sweet even cherubs weep
& Nereids float him in their seaweed boats…

Little one,
now you are mine—
sleep in my arms while I sing you this lullaby…
maybe you'll awaken in a kinder world

where children don't die at the edge of the sea.
Meanwhile, dream of peace
for this broken world.

T.J. Jarrett   Fort Comfort

*After M. Degas Teaches Art & Science at Durfee Intermediate
School, Detroit, 1942 by Philip Levine*

The nun stood by the chalkboard and
wrote the word America, underlined
it twice and asked: *What do you see here?*
Elizabeth shot up her hand and said:
*It is home. My grandmother came
here so that we could live.* The nun
asked the rest of the class: *Who else came?*
and the children shouted their countries
of origin. Except me. I was the only
black girl in the room and I stared off
toward the sea as I often did during
history class already imagining myself
far away from this place. The nun said:
Who else? And the children were quiet
and the nun said: *Some came in chains.*
They all looked at me, and I turned
my eyes back toward Fort Comfort
and imagined a ship docking there
and the cargo descending to the pier.
Rachel, a serious girl with brown eyes
which always appeared to be at the verge
of overflowing asked: *What happened
to the men before us?* The nun said:
We killed them, her voice wavering.

She cleared her throat. *We killed them,*
and she looked each of us in the eye.
I turned my eyes to the sea again, and
I could just make out the figure of
a woman waving to get my attention,
as if she knew me, as if my staring back
across the time, across the water meant
her survival, meant something. And the nun
went on and on about how nothing could
divide us and I wondered how long 400 years is,
how many bodies, how suffering was
multiplied among them, what is forever.

Toi Derricotte   Passing

A professor invites me to his "Black Lit" class; they're
reading Larson's *Passing*. One of the black
students says, "Sometimes light-skinned blacks
think they can fool other blacks,
but *I* can always tell," looking
right through me.
After I tell them I am black,
I ask the class, "Was I passing
when I was just sitting here,
before I told you?" A white woman
shakes her head desperately, as if
I had deliberately deceived her.
She keeps examining my face,
then turning away
as if she hopes I'll disappear. Why presume
"passing" is based on what I leave out
and not what she fills in?
In one scene in the book, in a restaurant,
she's "passing,"
though no one checked her at the door—
"Hey, you black?"
My father, who looked white,
told me this story: every year
when he'd go to get his driver's license,
the man at the window filling

out the form would ask,
"White or black?" pencil poised, without looking up.
My father wouldn't pass, but he might
use silence to trap a devil.
When he didn't speak, the man
would look up at my father's face.
"What did he write?"
my father quizzed me.

Howard Faerstein   The Baby in the Boat

Fleeing KIev's bleeding limbs,
whispering beneath the full moon's terror:

Throw him over
before someone thinks to check
why a baby is wailing
in the middle of the night.

Lake shadows rippling.
Mother biting her lips.

Eight of us want to live.
Throw him in now or I'll drown him myself

Wrestling off her youngest's pants
and there the open diaper pin
jabbing the fat flesh of her Abe
whose sobs heave to a whimpering halt;

then he sleeps and dreams
about the snow covering lawns in Buffalo
and his children, laughing,
burying themselves in it.

Howard Faerstein   **Godmother Goldie**

Such winter brilliance as was able to penetrate
the Crown Heights walk-up
in the kitchen in the small apartment
widowed Aunt Goldie now found herself in

& Goldie beamed brighter than Tycho's stella nova
when I placed the pizza box on the dinette table
for she had asked in her damaged Hungarian tongue
that I bring it to her, but secretly
so the orthodox caring for her
wouldn't know.

My uncle, the house painter, had hands that were meaty
but the rest of him shone like milk. His mother and siblings
neglected him, always referring to him as feeble-minded,
a simpleton, but Morris had a wife, Goldie,
who loved him and together they lived
on Mt. Eden Avenue. The family, what was left of it,
had fled the Zamechover shtetl in the Pale of Settlement,
escaping the pogroms years before the Nazis
exterminated the millions.

Today, in a museum in Santa Fe, I saw an exhibit
of Navajo spoons decorated with a swastika motif.
The curator's note read: *only the good and true
could wear swastika jewelry.* It was a sign of *great reverence.*
Then I remembered seeing Uncle Morris, my Russian
    godfather,
laid to rest in a Brooklyn chapel.
Goldie trudged down the aisle as her clan of Hungarians
called for a knife. Astride the coffin, she rent the fabric
covering her heart. In his casket, a squinty smile
steeplechasing his deeply lined face, Morris, a child of god,
looked so like a Navajo.

White, adopted from
the habits of subjects, her gown
was a British fashion sensation.

in the village of Beer near the sea, March to November,
    1840,
two hundred women sewed lace, her veil and flounce

to remain unique (patterns destroyed). Queen of the
United Kingdom of England, Ireland, Scotland and Wales

had her servants embroider chemise and split drawers
with a crown, number each to track its progress

through the laundry, her full name Alexandrina
Victoria after her godfather, Emperor of Russia.

She gave birth to nine children, among them a daughter
born November twenty-first, my birthday. I had blood

in Mother Russia. My Alexander grew tobacco
for the czar, sailed to New York, rolled Cuban cigars.

My grandmother tells me she rode with the czar,
wind whipped her hair, czarina was jealous,

she wiped out all the village Jews, czar could not
protect her. Leave, he said, and gave her a tobacco flower,

its sweet bud tucked behind her bride's ear.
Black her tresses, dark her dresses, easy to clean and go.

By the time we know her, she is screaming at us
for using the wrong spoons.

As soon as we start walking, she teaches us to deal poker,
drink coffee in milk, mouth words that could charm the
    BVDs

off Brooklyn Russkies. We too are charmed: we farm
    tobacco in Popov for
as long as we can imagine—

and Grandma, we too ride with art and royalty—
we too are the star in the czar's car.

Frederick Feirstein   Mulberry

Mulberry Street where Jill would go to shop
For olives, dried cod, freshly-killed veal chops.
It's San Genarro's Feast with tourists snacking
Calzone, Sicilian Pizza, smacking
Their stomachs, hearts, stretching their arteries
With candied apples and ricotta cheese
Sloshed down with red wine, white wine, cider, beer.
Here thoughts of 9/11 disappear
Down their digestive tracts they'll carry back
To Bay Ridge, Philly, Stamford, Hackensack.
Tonight this street will be a feast of lights,
Rose-colored. Oz-colored, yellow, blue and white,
With belting by Dean Martin, Pavorotti
And karioka by Lotte Wolf and Wild Coyote
And old men playing gin who smoke and cough,
Their drunken *moglies* taking "something off"
    —A scarf, a shawl they'll wrap around the face
—Like Muslim women, dancing with studied grace.
    I walk around them, out to Chinatown.
I'm in a maze. I have to get downtown,
Way past the Chinese mothers wielding mops
To chide their children who've been Westernized.
They're straight lines, dots—they're all apostrophized
Immigrants who've survived foul cargo ships
And spare ribs smeared with sweet and sour dips
And chickens burned to pimpled skin

And pretty peddlers burned by Time to crones
And old men, young men hawking watches, rings,
And lit-up Yo Yo's circling on white strings
Around The World, or Sleeping as we learned
When children, ignorant that towers burn
And crumble like tall parents unprepared
For what we dreamed of but we hadn't dared
To fully fantasize about. I sprint
To New York City's government
Buildings—The Court House, Police Plaza, City Hall
Where lawyers march, where vagrants slide down walls
Where Mayans play what sounds American
On tambourines and home-made pipes of Pan.

Lisken Van Pelt Dus   My Father Asks What I Remember

Scarf tied under my chin,
we walked through cemeteries,
through muddy fords, through
streets with cracks, through woods.

Once, someone was playing
a violin: I could see the notes
cascading from a high window,
their yellows, blues, reds

almost too much to bear,
but pretty—not like the shelling
that drowned me in oceans
of clashing color. Had I known then

that you didn't see sound, would I
have told you, Father? I don't know.
I bent and folded wild grasses
in my fingers as we walked.

Or rubbed a scrap of paper.
When the bats appeared, swiping
across our path, rest was coming.
Sometimes, even a pillow.

More often not. Cities
had subways, which felt safe
but when the buskers began,
the colors bounced off walls

and were blinding. At home,
there had been a lion in the zoo.
When I saw a toy one in a store window,
I said nothing, and we walked on.

Howard F. Stein

"Teeming shores,"
"wretched refuse,"
people in vast waves of flight.
They flee, they walk, they run,
they spill over edges of boats,
they float, they swim, they drown,
they seek refuge from endless hate and war,
many unwanted, many welcomed.

Who would have known
twelve years ago
lust for oil and obsession
with unseating a dictator
would lead to this,
worse fanaticism than before?
Rape, bloodshed, and destruction
on an unimaginable scale.
Après nous, le déluge,
the leaders seemed to say—
collateral damage.
In their single-minded ambition,
unintended consequences
do not matter.
Where have all the flower petals gone?

For those in flight, anything is
better than the life from which they run.
Then, the wager that
somewhere, by someone,
a door, a gate, would open;
they would be let in,
and months of flight
would finally end.
There would be the possibility
of settling into home again—
for most, still a dream.

Howard F. Stein   **Unclaimed**

I show up on your doorstep;
You decline even to greet me,
But only say, as your index finger
Points far away,
"You do not belong;
You are not from here;
You can never be
One of us."
I see in her eyes
and in her forearms,
tightly locked against her chest,
that she will never claim me
as related to her in any way.

Dejected, I turn to leave,
But say first to her,
Looking into her frozen face:
"I am the stranger
You once were—
And fear again to be.
You were unclaimed
And cannot recognize
Yourself once more in me."

Lisken Van Pelt Dus   Kwashiorkor

Entire villages meander from hunger to hunger
enticed by small scraps, the scrapings of a bowl
hallucinating meat and banquets on tables
savoring saliva in dreams between wakings
silencing the children with pebbles like sweets

Empty is the normal condition of the bowls
mothers place carefully on shelves behind basins
harvest failed again in sun's conspiracy with rain
bellies distended as if in mockery of my prosperity
each child weaned another body ballooning

Of the dreams of the fathers away working
I can say nothing except that they are also empty
cries of their children silent across the miles
open mouths turned upward like baby birds'
hunger eating the fathers too yes hunger

I was on my way to see my woman
but the Law said I was on my way
thru a red light red light red light
and if you saw my woman
you could understand
I was just being a man.
It wasn't about no light
it was about my ride
and if you saw my ride
you could dig that too, you dig?
Sunroof stereo radio black leather
bucket seats sit low you know,
the body's cool, but the tires are worn.
Ride when the hard time come, ride
when they're gone, in other words
the light was green.

I could wake up in the morning
without a warning
and my world could change:
blink your eyes.
All depends on the skin,
all depends on the skin you're living in.

Up the window comes the Law
with his hand on his gun
what's up? what's happening?
I said I guess
that's when I really broke the law.
He said *a routine. step out the car*
a routine, *assume the position.*
Put your hands up in the air
you know the routine, like you just don't care.
License and registration.
Deep was the night and the light
from the North Star on the car door, déjà vu
we've been through this before,
why did you stop me?
Somebody had to stop you.
I watch the news, you always lose.
You're unreliable, that's undeniable.
This is serious, you could be dangerous.

I could wake up in the morning
without a warning
and my world could change:
blink your eyes.
All depends, all depends on the skin,
all depends on the skin you're living in.

New York City, they got laws
can't no bruthas drive outdoors,
in certain neighborhoods, on particular streets
near and around certain types of people.
They got laws.
All depends, all depends on the skin,
all depends on the skin you're living in.

Her mother is crying
because Briana came home from school screaming in
   agony.
Two girls in her class are named Brianna
and the children distinguish them
by calling her "The Black Briana," taunting her.
She screams at her mother, "I don't want to be
"The Black Briana!"
Her mother weeps, helplessly. "What can I do?
I give her dolls, read her
black history. How can I protect her?"
Already at five the children understand,
"black" is not a color, it is a
blazing skin.

winter mornings, then the inner self begins, has to,
making a kind of light just ahead,
no way to see farther.

Anxiety's light.
Shining on the mothers of Damascus
as they watch their children begin to starve,

on our broken porch
needing to be fixed for a decade,
on the money I spent for our daughter's wedding dress,

winding inevitably back to the days, each one,
I was ashamed of the shabby,
ill-fitting hand-me-downs

Mother got for me at the church.
In a world where her dress shouldn't exist,
how stubbornly I want my daughter to have it.

2.

Mothers of Damascus, I've put us in this poem
together; yes, I do understand
the difference between hunger and hungers.

My imagination can't reach you, only claim
to know the hollow inside
when I am beyond tears.

I dream in fruit, one Syrian woman said,
according to our news. Like dreams,
words peel an orange and hand it to your daughter.

For your son, a luscious bowl of pomegranate seeds.
Plunging in the spoon,
he wreaths his mouth in them, that many.

3.

Unwilling to lie down
more than a certain number of hours,
you sit up and fear dawn.

I fix tea and oatmeal, shuffling in the kitchen.
Right before my daughter's wedding, my husband
has died.

Whatever dress she has, she won't
have him. Your husbands? I don't know.
Your children? I know.

Tomas Tranströmer
Translated by Patty Crane

Romanesque Arches

Inside the enormous Romanesque church, tourists
   crammed into the half-darkness.
Vault opening behind vault and no view of the whole.
Several candle flames flickered.
An angel without a face embraced me
and whispered through my whole body:
"Don't feel ashamed that you're human, be proud!
Inside you, vault behind vault opens endlessly.
You'll never be complete, and that's how it should be."
I was blind with tears
and driven out into the sun-simmering piazza
together with Mr. and Mrs. Jones, Mr. Tanaka and
   Signora Sabatini
and inside each of them vault behind vault opened
   endlessly.

Marilyn Chin   The Floral Apron

The woman wore a floral apron around her neck,
that woman from my mother's village
with a sharp cleaver in her hand.
She said, "What shall we cook tonight?
Perhaps these six tiny squid
lined up so perfectly on the block?"

She wiped her hand on the apron,
pierced the blade into the first.
There was no resistance,
no blood, only cartilage
soft as a child's nose. A last
iota of ink made us wince.

Suddenly, the aroma of ginger and scallion fogged our
    senses,
and we absolved her for that moment's barbarism.
Then she, an elder of the tribe,
without formal headdress, without elegance,
deigned to teach the younger
about the Asian plight.

And although we have traveled far
we would never forget that primal lesson
—on patience, courage, forbearance,
or how to love squid despite squid,
how to honor the village, the tribe,
that floral apron.

Witter Bynner

The Wall

How is it,
That you, whom I can never know,
My beloved,
Are a wall between me and those I have known well—
So that my familiars vanish
Farther than the blue roofs of Nankow
And are lost among the desert hills?

Rafael Campo

In English That Is Spanish

You'd never understand why I'm confused.
I'd give you explanations if I could:
I'd write in Spanish just this once except
My pen keeps making English from my thoughts.
I'd write from deserts, or from jungles, but
It's autumn and I can't ignore these flames,
I can't ignore the fact I'm not in Spain—
but one's surroundings aren't languages.
(I still wish for a rainy season, but my droughts
Go on and on.) I wish I'd been
In Spain just once, to watch the Englishmen
Wash up on shore, I wish I'd heard them learn
The Spanish of my ancestors. I'd write
In perfect English if I could. I'd write
A sonnet just like Lorca, I'd write *El Cid*;
My English would be Spanish-sounding, rhyme
Would be so effortless I'd make you cry.
I'd make you cry in languages begun
Before there were two countries in the world,
In languages you'd want to make exist,
So one grand poetry sufficed. I'd write
To you in English and in Spanish, and
You'd understand that immortality
Is really only going back in time
Through languages like fourth dimensions, rhymes
Like clocks, to when we were a single race,

A single human being crying out
For rain, or fire from the falling leaves,
With no one ready to misunderstand.

Countee Cullen

Once, riding in old Baltimore,
    Heart-filled, head-filled with glee,
I saw a Baltimorean
    Keep looking straight at me.

Now I was eight and very small,
    And he was no whit bigger,
And so I smiled, but he poked out
    His tongue and called me, 'Nigger.'

I saw the whole of Baltimore
    From May until December;
Of all the things that happened there
    That's all that I remember.

Lucille Clifton   Sorrow Song

for the eyes of the children,
the last to melt,
the last to vaporize,
for the lingering
eyes of the children, staring,
the eyes of the children of
buchenwald,
of viet nam and johannesburg,
for the eyes of the children
of middle passage,
for cherokee eyes, ethiopian eyes,
russian eyes, american eyes,
for all that remains of the children,
their eyes,
staring at us, amazed to see
the extraordinary evil in
ordinary men.

William Stafford   **The Little Girl by the Fence at School**

Grass that was moving found all shades of brown,
moved them along, flowed autumn away
galloping southward where summer had gone.

And that was the morning someone's heart stopped
and all became still. A little girl said, "Forever?"
And the grass, "Yes. Forever." While the sky—

The sky — the sky — the sky.

Play like you had a war. Hardly anyone
got killed except thousands of the enemy,
and many go around starving, holding
their hands out in pictures, begging.

Their houses, even the concrete and iron,
they've disappeared. These people
now live camped in the open. Overhead
stars keep telling their old, old story.

You have this world. You wander the earth.
You can't live in a room.

Gwendolyn Brooks

I Am a Black

Kojo

According to my Teachers,
I am now an African-American.

They call me out of my name.

BLACK is an open umbrella.
I am Black and A Black forever.

I am one of The Blacks.

We are Here, we are There.
We occur in Brazil, in Nigeria, Ghana,
in Botswana, Tanzania, in Kenya,
in Russia, Australia, in Haiti, Soweto,
in Grenada, in Cuba, in Panama, Libya,
in England and Italy, France.

We are graces in any places.
I am Black and A Black
forever.

I am other than Hyphenation.

I say, proudly, MY PEOPLE!
I say proudly, OUR PEOPLE!
Our People do not disdain to eat yams or melons or
     grits
or to put peanut butter in stew.

I am Kojo. In West Afrika Kojo
means Unconquerable. My parents
named me the seventh day from my birth
in Black spirit, Black faith, Black communion.
I am Kojo. I am a Black.
And I Capitalize my name.

Do not call me out of my name.

Sir John Betjeman

False Security

I remember the dread with which I at a quarter past four
Let go with a bang behind me our house front door
And, clutching a present for my dear little hostess tight,
Sailed out for the children's party into the night
Or rather the gathering night. For still some boys
in the near municipal acres were making a noise
Shuffling in fallen leaves and shouting and whistling
And running past hedges of hawthorn spiky and bristling.
And black in the oncoming darkness stood out the trees
And pink shone the ponds in the sunset ready to freeze.
And all was still and ominous waiting for dark
And the keeper was ringing his closing bell in the park
And the arc lights started to fizzle and burst into mauve
As I climbed West Hill to the great big house in the grove,
Where the children's party was and the dear little hostess.
But halfway up stood the empty house where the ghost is.
I crossed to the other side and under the arc
Made a rush for the next kind lamppost out of the dark
And so to the next and the next till I reached the top
Where the grove branched off to the left. Then ready to
    drop
I ran to the ironwork gateway of number seven
Secure at last on the lamp lit fringe of heaven.
Oh who can say how subtle and safe one feels
Shod in one's children's sandals from Daniel Neal's?
Clad in one's party clothes made of stuff from Heal's?
And who can still one's thrill at the candle shine

On cakes and ices and jelly and blackcurrant wine.
And the warm little feel of my hostess's hand in mine?
And wasn't I proud that I was the last to go?
Too overexcited and pleased with myself to know
That the words I heard my hostess's mother employ
To a guest departing would ever diminish my joy.
I WONDER WHERE JULIA FOUND THAT
STRANGE, RATHER COMMON LITLE BOY?

Jimmy Santiago Baca   **The Day I Am Freed**

When I walk through the internment camp I am Gandhi,
when I walk through the door I am Che,
(in my heart I say it louder now)
when I walk through the door
I throw my worries away, I let my frustrations go,
all ill-will I have for others I let go,
I brush my sleeves of the uncertainties of yesterday,
when I walk through that door
if someone should ask you
tell them I am Ali
tell them I am Cesar Chavez,
when I walk through that door,
when I take a step forward, when I turn the corner
tell the world should they ask
I am who I dream myself,
(my heart cries louder and louder, with passion!)
tell them there goes the poet, there goes the painter,
tell all the haters and racists and cynics
I will not let them influence how I see myself,
that I am shaped by the loving hands of a dream,
no one makes me as they wish,
tell them please from conference halls and classrooms
from every street corner and market where you meet,
tell them you have seen me and talked to me
and that I am whom I dream myself to be—
when I opened my eyes this morning

I surrendered to my greatness,
I knelt down
and opened my arms to embrace my full being,
my potential to be who I am in this world—
leader, teacher, activist, tell them I no longer am
the woman they knew, that I have
found a way to love myself—
I closed my eyes,
and when I opened them,
I know that when I walk through that door
I am
Mother Teresa, Zapata, Anzaldua, Betita, Sor Juana,
Celia Cruz, Menchu…
because the day is young and I've got mountains to move,
mountains to move

Naomi Shihab Nye   **Mediterranean Blue**

If you are the child of a refugee, you do not
sleep easily when they are crossing the sea
on small rafts and you know they can't swim.
My father couldn't swim either. He swam through
sorrow, though, and made it to the other side
on a ship, pitching his old clothes overboard
at landing, then tried to be happy, make a new life.
But something inside him was always paddling home,
clinging to anything that floated—a story, a food, or face.
They are the bravest people on earth right now,
don't dare look down on them. Each mind a universe
swirling as many details as yours, as much love
for a humble place. Now the shirt is torn,
the sea too wide for comfort, and nowhere
to receive a letter for a very long time.

And if we can reach out a hand, we better.

Adrienne Rich   **Prospective Immigrants Please Note**

Either you will
go through this door
or you will not go through.

If you go through
there is always the risk
of remembering your name.

Things look at you doubly
and you must look back
and let them happen.

If you do not go through
it is possible
to live worthily

to maintain your attitudes
to hold your position
to die bravely

but much will blind you,
much will evade you,
at what cost who knows?

The door itself
Makes no promises.
It is only a door.

Gary Snyder   **How Poetry Comes to Me**

It comes blundering over the
Boulders at night, it stays
Frightened outside the
Range of my campfire
I go to meet it at the
Edge of the light

Marilyn Chin   We Are Americans Now, We Live in the Tundra

Today in hazy San Francisco, I face seaward
Toward China, a giant begonia—

Pink, fragrant, bitten
by verdigris and insects, I sing her

A blues song; even a Chinese girl gets the blues,
Her reticence is black and blue.

Let's sing about the extinct
Bengal tigers, about giant Pandas—

"Ling Ling loves Xing Xing—yet,
we will not mate. We are

Not impotent, we are important.
We blame the environment, we blame the zoo!"

What shall we plant for the future?
Bamboo, sassafras, coconut palms? No!

Legumes, wheat, maize, old swine
To milk the new.

We are Americans now, we live in the tundra
Of the Logical, a sea of cities, a wood of cars.

Farewell my ancestors:
Hirsute Taoists, failed scholars, farewell

My wetnurse, who feared and loathed the Catholics,
Who called out

> Now that half-men have occupied Canton
> Hide your daughters, lock your doors!

Witter Bynner   **Defeat**

On a train in Texas German prisoners eat
With white American soldiers, seat by seat,
While black American soldiers sit apart.
The white men eating meat, the black men heart.
Now, with that other war a century done.
Not the live North but the dead South has won.
Not yet a riven nation comes awake.
Whom are we fighting this time, for God's sake?
Mark well the token of the separate seat.
It is again ourselves whom we defeat.

Maria Mazziotti Gillan   I Was the Girl Who Never Spoke

I was the girl who never spoke, the shy girl,
my head perpetually bent, my eyes averted. The other night
at the bookstore I see the new Dick and Jane books
on a display shelf, I immediately remember how much

I wanted to be part of that Dick and Jane world,
the big white house, the huge lawn, the upper middle
class father with his cardigan and pipe. In first grade
I loved to look at the pictures in those readers,

the books offering me a window into a world
so different from my own Italian neighborhood,
the streets of Riverside lined with two or three family
shingled houses, statues of the Virgin Mary in a grotto

in the front yards of the newer hilltop houses, no front
yard at all in the ones like ours, roses climbing trellises,
vegetable gardens crammed full of corn and tomatoes,
zucchini and peppers, fig trees, grape vines.

In first grade I didn't know that the distance
between Jane's big white colonial and our apartment
could be traced in more than miles.

I was the girl who never spoke, afraid
I'd speak in Italian instead of English,
afraid, as I am sometimes even today,
that some expression common to Riverside
or some way of pronouncing a word will let everyone
    know

where I come from
where I belong
where I can never go.

Mark Smith-Soto   Accent

Fifty years ago my older brother brought home
the first tape recorder I'd ever seen, a little box
that pulled my voice out of the air and spun it back
transformed, whiny, stuffed-nose, singsong.
I stared at Dave. Could that be how I really sounded?
Like Speedy Gonzales, the cartoon mouse? He just
pressed a button and played it again, trying not to grin.

From then on, I obsessed over my pronunciation,
labored to distinguish *beach* from *bitch*
and *bum* from *bomb*, so no one would wonder
where I learned my English. *Where are you from?*
how much it meant to me to avoid that question!
For years I practiced until I spoke like a proper Yankee,
not a refugee from the Central American wars.

Or so I thought. Then a clerk at Stop-N-Go asked if I
came from Pakistan: he said I talked just like his dentist.
At least, I thought, he isn't thinking *Spic*.
Time to make peace with what could not be fixed.

This morning I listen to myself on my iPhone,
rehearsing a poem I will read tonight, and catch
in my tone a lilt that's gently foreign,

like a distant song.

1.

AEGEAN BLUES

The sea is for holidaymakers, summer on the beach,
Surely there is space enough to spread a towel for each;
Dry land isn't something you should pray to reach.

Look how glad our kids are, making their sandy town,
And how they build the battlements the laughing waves
    tear down.
But it's the selfsame water, where some swim, and others
    drown.

The sea is full of dangers, the shallows and the deep.
The sea is full of treasures, down there five fathoms deep,
The sea is full of salt: there are no more tears to weep.

The ferryman says we cross tonight; and everyone pays
    cash.
Charon don't take Mastercard, you have to pay him cash.
The water seems so calm tonight, you hardly hear the
    splash.

There was a boy named Icarus; old Daedalus's son.
He turned into a waxwing, black against the sun.
Drowned because he tried to fly. (He's not the only one.)

Why would a kid lie in the sand, and not take off his shoes?
Why would he lie there facedown, the color of a bruise?
The sea can make you carefree, nothing left to lose.

There's indigo and turquoise, there's cobalt, sapphire, navy,
And there's a dark like wine, my love, out where things get
    wavy.
Listen, that's the worry note, reminds me of my baby.

2.

CHARON

When some, as promised, made it to dry land,
He profited, high and dry, but others, owing
To fickle winds, or a puncture, or freak waves,
Arrived at a farther shore, another beach
Lapped by a numb forgetting, still in the clothes
Someone had washed and pressed to face the day,
And lay in attitudes much like repose.
And Charon made a killing either way,
Per child alone, 600 euros each.

Yehuda Amichai   And the Migration of My Parents

And the migration of my parents
Has not subsided in me. My blood goes on sloshing
Between my ribs, long after the vessel has come to rest.
And the migration of my parents has not subsided in me.
Winds of long time over stones. Earth
Forgets the steps of those who trod her.
Terrible fate. Patches of a conversation after midnight.
Win and lose. Night recalls and day forgets.
My eyes looked long into a vast desert
And were calmed a bit. A woman. Rules of a game
I was not taught. Laws of pain and burden.
My heart barely ekes out the bread
Of its daily love. My parents in their migration.
On Mother Earth, I am always an orphan.
Too young to die, too old to play.
The weary hewer and the empty quarry in one body.
Archaeology of the future, repositories
Of what was not. And the migration of my parents
Has not subsided in me. From bitter nations I have learned
Bitter tongues for my silence
Among these houses, always like ships.
And my veins and my sinews, a thicket
Of ropes I cannot unravel. And then
My death and an end to the migration of my parents.

Kalpana Asok   Raw

The look that lingers
Fractions too long
The look
that passes
Over and through
The too-quickly
Averted eyes.

How do you speak
so Well
so exotic
so spiritual
so calm
Where Learn it
Were you
born with it?

Do you know
Slough and Slough?
You do ?
Ahhh … okay
Now I can use it
In my verse
And worse
For everyone.

Richard Blanco

To love a country as if you've lost one: 1968,
my mother leaves Cuba for America, a scene
I imagine as if standing in her place—one foot
inside a plane destined for a country she knew
only as a name, a color on a map, or glossy photos
from drugstore magazines, her other foot anchored
to the platform of her *patria*, her hand clutched
around one suitcase, taking only what she needs
most: hand-colored photographs of her family,
her wedding veil, the doorknob of her house,
a jar of dirt from her backyard, goodbye letters
she won't open for years. The sorrowful drone
of engines, one last, deep breath of familiar air
she'll take with her, one last glimpse at all
she'd ever known: the palm trees wave goodbye
as she steps onto the plane, the mountains shrink
from her eyes as she lifts off into another life.

To love a country as if you've lost one: I hear her
—*once upon a time*—reading picture books
over my shoulder at bedtime, both of us learning
English, sounding out words as strange as the talking
animals and fair-haired princesses in their pages.
I taste her first attempts at macaroni-n-cheese
(but with chorizo and peppers), and her shame
over Thanksgiving turkeys always dry, but countered

by her perfect pork *pernil* and garlic *yucca.* I smell
the rain of those mornings huddled as one under
one umbrella waiting for the bus to her ten-hour days
at the cash register. At night the *zzz-zzz* of her sewing
her own blouses, *quinceañera* dresses for her nieces
still in Cuba, guessing at their sizes, and the gowns
she'd sell to neighbors to save for a rusty white sedan—
no hubcaps, no air-conditioning, sweating all the way
through our first vacation to Florida theme parks.

To love a country as if you've lost one: as if
it were you on a plane departing from America
forever, clouds closing like curtains on your country,
the last scene in which you're a madman scribbling
the names of your favorite flowers, trees, and birds
you'd never see again, the color of your father's eyes,
your mother's hair, terrified you could forget these.
To love a country as if I was my mother last spring
hobbling, insisting I help her climb all the way up
to the U.S. Capitol, as if she were here before you today
instead of me, explaining her tears, cheeks pink
as the cherry blossoms coloring the air that day when
she stopped, turned to me, and said: You know, *mijo,*
it isn't where you're born that matters, it's where
you choose to die—that's your country.

Ruth Awad   **My Father Dreams of a New Country**

Lebanon, 1978

America, I see through your glass—
I reach my hand and my fingerprints
are everywhere. Like leaves the gust blows in.

I don't have money to feed your fountains
or enough water that it's never a wish,

but America, I can't stop drinking you in.
Your trains, their freight like hours,
like the vowels cut from my name.

When will you learn my name?

I'm running to you but I can't get there
fast enough. I'm strung up on gridirons
and city lights. Aren't my arms tired of reaching?

Isn't my back tired of carrying this night around?
Be good to me like a summer rain, I swear I'm burning.

Coming from home, and home being far away from the
    home that I know,
a package weighing several pounds arrived at my door.
I had no idea, no concept, no thought of what this was for
or why it had come as it did, via expensive and intimate
    courier
in private truck with uniformed handler—for pomp and
    for show
instead of for practical, sensible use of a hurrier—
a way to deliver a package from *"home"*—the foreign one I
    once knew.

Orphaned at ten, raised by few relatives hated at once and
    forever,
with no possessions of my own—to call my own—
a package arriving without any reason recalled the one
    time I had known
the joy of a gift, unanticipated, fallen at my feet and
    delighting
the child I was then. I remained that distant, foreign child,
    for no endeavor
with a box could have contained the remnants of the life I
    was citing
to the resistant walls and the hard-bolted door that the
    fates drew.

I wouldn't lift the carton from its place just barely in my
    house.
I hadn't read the label, hadn't noticed who had sent the
    thing
until I noticed on one edge, attached with tape to shield a
    ding,
a paper plate whose borders were the same as for my
    birthday fete
the year that I turned nine—my Polish death to come—
    this lowly city mouse
by every stranger to watch as I my candles blew.

Delivered isn't quite the same as deliverance to this world.
And no amount of pressure could persuade me to be
    opening
this box that sat there on my floor and left me wishing,
    praying, hoping,
it contained the one and only present I had ever truly
    cherished.
Then, when at last I cut the tape, removed the paper, and
    had hurled
away the rubbish I was faced with what, my whole life
    long, I'd missed:
my mother's wedding gown, her best prized thing, so
    sweet and true.

She'd worn it for me every year upon the anniversary date
of when she'd wed and then conceived the son she loved
  throughout her life;
those last ten years when she was forced to face the world
  away and all its strife
a grieving widow had to bear. It made her ill and so unable
to recover what she'd known for years with her own
  soulmate.
And now for me this became a gift to make my own
  world stable
sent by folks I'd hated all my life who were related and
  were relatively few.

  That hate should mate with sympathy from overseas,
  while overwrought gentility was, now at forty-five,
  a world away from any love I'd bought.

He gossips like my grandmother, this man
with my face, and I could stand
amused all afternoon
in the Hon Kee Grocery,
amid hanging meats he
chops: roast pork cut
from a hog hung
by nose and shoulders,
her entire skin burnt
crisp, flesh I know
to be sweet,
her shining
face grinning
up at ducks
dangling single file,
each pierced by black
hooks through breast, bill,
and steaming from a hole
stitched shut at the ass.
I step to the counter, recite,
and he, without even slightly
varying the rhythm of his current confession or harangue,
scribbles my order on a greasy receipt,
and chops it up quick.

Such a sorrowful Chinese face,
nomad, Gobi, Northern

in its boniness
clear from the high
warlike forehead
to the sheer edge of the jaw.
He could be my brother, but finer,
and, except for his left forearm, which is engorged,
sinewy from his daily grip and
wield of a two-pound tool,
he's delicate, narrow-
waisted, his frame
so slight a lover, some
rough other
might break it down
its smooth, oily length.
In his light-handed calligraphy
on receipts and in his
moodiness, he is
a Southerner from a river-province;
suited for scholarship, his face poised
above an open book, he'd mumble
his favorite passages.
He could be my grandfather;
come to America to get a Western education
in 1917, but too homesick to study,
he sits in the park all day, reading poems
and writing letters to his mother.

He lops the head off, chops
the neck of the duck
into six, slits
the body
open, groin
to breast, and drains
the scalding juices,
then quarters the carcass
with two fast hacks of the cleaver,
old blade that has worn
into the surface of the round
foot-thick chop-block
a scoop that cradles precisely the curved steel.

The head, flung from the body, opens
down the middle where the butcher
cleanly halved it between
the eyes, and I
see, foetal-crouched
inside the skull, the homunculus,
gray brain grainy
to eat.
Did this animal, after all, at the moment
its neck broke,
image the way his executioner
shrinks from his own death?

Is this how
I, too, recoil from my day?
See how this shape
hordes itself, see how
little it is.
See its grease on the blade.
Is this how I'll be found
when judgement is passed, when names
are called, when crimes are tallied?
This is also how I looked before I tore my mother open.
Is this how I presided over my century, is this how
I regarded the murders?
This is also how I prayed.
Was it me in the Other
I prayed to when I prayed?
This too was how I slept, clutching my wife.
Was it me in the other I loved
when I loved another?
The butcher sees me eye this delicacy.
With a finger, he picks it
out of the skull-cradle
and offers it to me.
I take it gingerly between my fingers
and suck it down.
I eat my man.

The noise the body makes
when the body meets
the soul over the soul's ocean and penumbra
is the old sound of up-and-down, in-and-out,
a lump of muscle chug-chugging blood
into the ear; a lover's
heart-shaped tongue;
flesh rocking flesh until flesh comes;
the butcher working
at his block and blade to marry their shapes
by violence and time;
an engine crossing,
re-crossing salt water, hauling
immigrants and the junk
of the poor. These
are the faces I love, the bodies
and scents of bodies
for which I long
in various ways, at various times,
thirteen gathered around the redwood,
happy, talkative, voracious
at day's end,
eager to eat
four kinds of meat
prepared four different ways,
numerous plates and bowls of rice and vegetables,

each made by distinct affections
and brought to table by many hands.

Brothers and sisters by blood and design,
who sit in separate bodies of varied shapes,
we constitute a many-membered
body of love.
In a world of shapes
of my desires, each one here
is a shape of one of my desires, and each
is known to me and dear by virtue
of each one's unique corruption
of those texts, the face, the body:
that jut jaw
to gnash tendon;
that wide nose to meet the blows
a face like that invites;
those long eyes closing on the seen;
those thick lips
to suck the meat of animals
or recite 300 poems of the T'ang;
these teeth to bite my monosyllables;
these cheekbones to make
those syllables sing the soul.
Puffed or sunken
according to the life,

dark or light according
to the birth, straight
or humped, whole, manqué, quasi, each pleases, verging
on utter grotesquery.
All are beautiful by variety.
The soul too
is a debasement
of a text, but, thus, it
acquires salience, although a
human salience, but
inimitable, and, hence, memorable.
God is the text.
The soul is a corruption
and a mnemonic.

A bright moment,
I hold up an old head
from the sea and admire the haughty
down-curved mouth
that seems to disdain
all the eyes are blind to,
including me, the eater.
Whole unto itself, complete
without me, yet its
shape complements the shape of my mind.
I take it as text and evidence
of the world's love for me,

and I feel urged to utterance,
urged to read the body of the world, urged
to say it
in human terms,
my reading a kind of eating, my eating
a kind of reading,
my saying a diminishment, my noise
a love-in-answer.

What is it in me would
devour the world to utter it?
What is it in me will not let
the world be, would eat
not just this fish,
but the one who killed it,
the butcher who cleaned it.
I would eat the way he
squats, the way he
reaches into the plastic tubs
and pulls out a fish, clubs it, takes it
to the sink, guts it, drops it on the weighing pan.
I would eat that thrash
and plunge of the watery body
in the water, that liquid violence
between the man's hands,
I would eat

the gutless twitching on the scales,
three pounds of dumb
nerve and pulse, I would eat it all
to utter it.
The deaths at the sinks, those bodies prepared
for eating, I would eat,
and the standing deaths
at the counters, in the aisles,
the walking deaths in the streets,
the death-far-from-home, the death-
in-a-strange-land, these Chinatown
deaths, these American deaths.
I would devour this race to sing it,
this race that according to Emerson
managed to preserve to a hair
for three or four thousand years
the ugliest features in the world.
I would eat these features, eat
the last three or four thousand years, every hair.
And I would eat Emerson, his transparent soul, his
soporific transcendence.
I would eat this head,
glazed in pepper-speckled sauce,
the cooked eyes opaque in their sockets.
I bring it to my mouth and—
the way I was taught, the way I've watched
others before me do—

with a stiff tongue lick out
the cheek-meat and the meat
over the armored jaw, my eating,
its sensual, salient nowness,
punctuating the void
from which such hunger springs and to which it proceeds.

And what
is this
I excavate
with my mouth?
What is this
plated, ribbed, hinged
architecture, this *carp head*,
but one more
articulation of a single nothing
severally manifested?
What is my eating,
rapt as it is,
but another
shape of going,
my immaculate expiration?

O, nothing is so
steadfast it won't go
the way the body goes.
The body goes.
The body's grave,
so serious
in its dying,
arduous as martyrs
in that task and as
glorious. It goes
empty always
and announces its going
by spasms and groans, farts and sweats.

What I thought were the arms
aching *cleave*, were the knees trembling *leave*.
What I thought were the muscles
insisting *resist, persist, exist,*
were the pores
hissing *mist* and *waste*.
What I thought was the body humming *reside, reside,*
was the body sighing *revise, revise*.
O, the murderous deletions, the keening
down to nothing, the cleaving.
All of the body's revisions end
in death.
All of the body's revisions end.

Bodies eating bodies, heads eating heads,
we are nothing eating nothing,
and though we feast,
are filled, overfilled,
we go famished.
We gang the doors of death.
That is, our deaths are fed
that we may continue our daily dying,
our bodies going
down, while the plates-soon-empty
are passed around, that true
direction of our true prayers,
while the butcher spells
his message, manifold,
in the mortal air.
He coaxes, cleaves, brings change
before our very eyes, and at every
moment of our being.
As we eat we're eaten.
Else what is this
violence, this salt, this
passion, this heaven?

I thought the soul an airy thing.
I did not know the soul
is cleaved so that the soul might be restored.

Live wood hewn,
its sap springs from a sticky wound.
No seed, no egg has he
whose business calls for an axe.
In the trade of my soul's shaping,
he traffics in hews and hacks.

No easy thing, violence.
One of its names? Change. Change
resides in the embrace
of the effaced and the effacer,
in the covenant of the opened and the opener;
the axe accomplishes it on the soul's axis.
What then may I do
but cleave to what cleaves me.
I kiss the blade and eat my meat.
I thank the wielder and receive,
while terror spirits
my change, sorrow also.
The terror the butcher
scripts in the unhealed
air, the sorrow of his Shang
dynasty face,
African face with slit eyes. He is
my sister, this
beautiful Bedouin, this Shulamite,
keeper of sabbaths, diviner

of holy texts, this dark
dancer, this Jew, this Asian, this one
with the Cambodian face, Vietnamese face, this Chinese
I daily face,
this immigrant,
this man with my own face.

Leroy V. Quintana

What It Was Like

If you want to know what
it was like, I'll tell you
what my *tio* told me.
There was a truck driver,
Antonio, who could handle a
rig as easily in reverse as
anybody else straight ahead.

Too bad he's a Mexican was
what my *tio* said the
Anglos had to say
about that.

And thus the moral:

Where do you begin if
you begin with if
you're too good
it's too bad?

If only you had written our language
we would have remembered how you died

If you had wakened at our windows
we would have known who you were

we would have felt horror
at the pictures of you behind barbed wire

from which you did not emerge
we would have returned to the shots of you lying dead
    with your kin

we would have ached to hear of your freezing
and your hunger in the hands of your own kind

we would have suffered at the degradation of your women
we would have studied you reverently

we would have repeated the words of your children
we would have been afraid for you

you would have made us ashamed and indignant
and righteous

we would have been proud of you
we would have mourned you

you would have survived
as we do

we might have believed
in a homeland

Gerald Stern   The Dancing

In all these rotten shops, in all this broken furniture
and wrinkled ties and baseball trophies and coffee pots
I have never seen a postwar Philco
with the automatic eye
nor heard Ravel's "Bolero" the way I did
in 1945 in that tiny living-room
on Beechwood Boulevard, nor danced as I did
then, my knives all flashing, my hair all streaming,
my mother red with laughter, my father cupping
his left hand under his armpit, doing the dance
of old Ukraine, the sound of his skin half drum,
half fart, the world at last a meadow,
the three of us whirling and singing, the three of us
screaming and falling, as if we were dying,
as if we could never stop—in 1945—
in Pittsburgh, beautiful filthy Pittsburgh, home
of the evil Mellons, 5,000 miles away
from the other dancing—in Poland and Germany—
oh God of mercy, oh wild God.

Michael Waters

Sophie Rose

Kristallnacht, 1938/2015

Vestal light, zenithal light, light tarnished
Only as it falls above tarred rooftops,
Tinged with ginger;
                        thistly, synagogal
Light glimpsed in mute rapport with its maker—
How she loves to gaze long into the light.
Whosoever enters into this light
Censures history, its peals of breaking
Glass, encroaching darkness, human din, charred
Trees, *whosoever leans into this light*
As into breath burdened with prayer: that child
Who glances over her father's shoulder
To hold fast her neighbors, her house, its plumes
Of smoke like the smudged tableau of mottled
Coats commingling scents of wet wool and fear:
That child will cling to the one bearing her
Until she falls asleep, before transport,
Among the dispossessed in the rail yard…
To awaken slowly in this foreign
Country, last name scraped smooth, to inhabit
The crepe skin of perpetual grief, while
Beyond pinned-open drapes sleet rinses scarred
Sycamores struggling to breathe, to grasp light
Curling chimneys above Queens Boulevard…
So she rises, surprised again to be
Not quite dead, to sponge away sleep's barbed grains,
To boil eggs, to turn loud the Rachael Ray,
And to salt the dough for our daily bread.

Mihaela Moscaliuc   Refugee Song

Sixteen lost at sea survived
at her breast.

When her mind tangled in sea grass,
lips kept the milk flowing:
dying women, men, ghostling of newborn
afloat among damselfish.

The shore pushed them back
toward lands poisoned by war.
The milk ran out of bodies.

Father, all you ever did
was gorge on my flesh.

My belly grew eyes
but the pelvis shrank,

thinned by vinegar
and grazing nails.

What am I to call
your hunger,

the teeth marks
clotted with milk,

the shore I barely reached?

Jane Kenyon   Here

You always belonged here.
You were theirs, certain as a rock.
I'm the one who worries
if I fit in with the furniture
and the landscape.

          But I "follow too much
the devices and desires of my own heart."

Already the curves in the road
are familiar to me, and the mountain
in all kinds of light,
treating all people the same.
And when I come over the hill,
I see the house, with its generous
and firm proportions, smoke
rising gaily from the chimney.

I feel my life start up again,
like a cutting when it grows
the first pale and tentative
root hair in a glass of water.

Fady Joudah

Dehiscence

I forgot to say goodbye to the kids.
I knelt into my weeping until my heart
broke me awake. My forehead
touched the floor. If dream is memory
I was captured in a van, incarcerated. I was
and wasn't a leader. The prison
was a camp in the wilderness. Its warden
was kind. Unkindness came
from the rules, which came from behind
desert mountains. I didn't say goodbye
to my kids. We were watching a soccer game
when it happened. My boyhood
team is a city's that was steeped in shipping
slaves, but that's long ago now. Two
of the goal scorers were Muslim.
One Senegalese, the other Turkish
who would have us believe he's German.
I didn't say goodbye to the kids.
I sobbed, I shook. I woke up with a dry face
and a cloven heart. I uttered the Arabic word
for it. There's a world out there, people
no less beautiful than you are.
I stayed in bed for an hour, less water
with time. I recalled the moment

No more his little boy I parted
with a tenderness that wouldn't
visit me the same again. I felt
his acceptance unaware he'd begun waiting
for mine. It was after lunch. We were
on the couch. He stroked my hair, neck,
and forearm. It felt good, then I felt older.
Slowly, I got up, walked away, his fingers
trailing the air of my wake. Both of us
wordless. I didn't say goodbye to my kids.
There's a world out there, people
who don't ask me what I'm about to say.
You're not time. I served with time
and you're not it.

One of the things my father never liked about me was
my dark skin. *You used to be so pretty*, was the way
he'd put it, and it was true, there is proof, a baby
picture of a curly-haired, just a hair's breadth away
from fair-skinned child, my small fingers balled
up into fists.

And then, as if some God shrugged and suddenly
turned away its gaze, something caved in, and I was
dark, dark, and all that it implied.

So what happened? My father always seemed to
want me to explain, what did this desertion mean?
This skin that seemed born to give up, this hair that
crinkled to knots, this fairy-tale-like transformation?

You used to look real good, my father, a man of
slightly lighter hue, would say to me, his son, his
changeling. *Maybe you ought to wash more.*

Yehuda Amichai   The Diameter of the Bomb

The diameter of the bomb was thirty centimeters
and the diameter of its effective range about seven meters.
with four dead and eleven wounded.
And around these, in a larger circle
of pain and time, two hospitals are scattered
and one graveyard. But the young woman
who was buried in the city she came from
at a distance of more than a hundred kilometers
enlarges the circle considerably,
and the solitary man mourning her death
at the distant shores of a country far across the sea
includes the entire world in the circle.
And I won't even mention the howl of the orphans
that reaches up to the throne of God and
beyond, making a circle with no end and no God.

Translated by Chana Block and Stephen Mitchell

Martín Espada **Ode to the Soccer Ball Sailing Over a Barbed Wire Fence**

Tornillo ... has become the symbol of what may be the largest U.S. mass detention of children not charged with crimes since the World War II internment of Japanese-Americans. –Robert Moore, Texas Monthly

Praise *Tornillo:* word for *screw* in Spanish, word for *jailer*
    in English,
word for three thousand adolescent migrants incarcerated
    in camp.

Praise the three thousand soccer balls gift-wrapped at
    Christmas,
as if raindrops in the desert inflated and bounced through
    the door.

Praise the soccer games rotating with a whistle every
    twenty minutes
so three thousand adolescent migrants could take turns
    kicking a ball.

Praise the boys and girls who walked a thousand miles,
    blood caked
in their toes, yelling in Spanish and a dozen Mayan
    tongues on the field.

Praise the first teenager, brain ablaze like chili pepper
   Christmas lights,
to kick a soccer ball high over the chain link and barbed
   wire fence.

Praise the first teenager to scrawl a name and number on
   the face
of the ball, then boot it all the way to the dirt road on the
   other side.

Praise the smirk of teenagers at the jailers scooping up
   fugitive
soccer balls, jabbering about the ingratitude of teenagers
   at Christmas.

Praise the soccer ball sailing over the barbed wire fence,
   white
and black like the moon, yellow like the sun, blue like the
   world.

Praise the soccer ball flying to the moon, flying to the sun,
   flying to other
worlds, flying to Antigua Guatemala, where Starbucks
   buys coffee beans.

Praise the soccer ball bounding off the lawn at the White
    House,
thudding off the president's head as he waves to absolutely
    no one.

Praise the piñata of the president's head, jellybeans
    pouring from his ears,
enough to free three thousand adolescents incarcerated at
    Tornillo.

Praise *Tornillo:* word in Spanish for adolescent migrant
    internment camp,
abandoned by jailers in the desert, liberated by a blizzard
    of soccer balls.

Galway Kinnell   **Prayer**

Whatever happens. Whatever
what *is* is is what
I want. Only that. But that.

David Giannini   ## Tikkun Olam (Repairing the World)

16th century CE–present time

We were talking about 'the Ari,' that ancient
rabbi envisioning his god-as-infinite-light
creating the world by withholding his breath

to make darkness, then exhaling
ten holy vague vessels, each filled
with primordial light, each then breaking

apart to make things and beings, our job forever
to develop enough within ourselves to heal
the world, to strive to retrieve the broken

and restore to indivisible origin—wind-whipped
cones and needles thrown down from pines
strew our lawn and driveway, shaded trunks

spalted by wet summer—divisible light
and contraction; and since other things
and mammals must restore, too, what do

they do? What does a stone do? We turn
to each other in the dark, and sometimes feel
the wounds of a memory made of stinging light.

Danusha Lameris   Small Kindnesses

I've been thinking about the way, when you walk
down a crowded aisle, people pull in their legs
to let you by. Or how strangers still say "bless you"
when someone sneezes, a leftover
from the Bubonic plague. "Don't die," we are saying.
And sometimes, when you spill lemons
from your grocery bag, someone else will help you
pick them up. Mostly, we don't want to harm each other.
We want to be handed our cup of coffee hot,
and to say thank you to the person handing it. To smile
at them and for them to smile back. For the waitress
to call us honey when she sets down the bowl of clam
    chowder,
and for the driver in the red pick-up truck to let us pass.
We have so little of each other, now. So far
from tribe or fire. Only these brief moments of exchange.
What if they are the true dwelling of the holy, these
fleeing temples we make together when we say, "Here,
have my seat," "Go ahead—you first," "I like your hat."

Notes on Contributors

JUSTEN AHREN is Martha's Vineyard Poet Laureate, and founder of Noepe Center for Literary Arts and The Italy Writing Workshop in Orvieto, Italy. He has published two collections of poetry, "A Strange Catechism" and "A Machine for Remembering," a collection of poems and photographs drawn from stories of refugees he heard while volunteering on Lesvos, Greece and following refugee routes in Europe.

JULIA ALVAREZ's stories, essays and poems have appeared in many well-known publications, including *The New Yorker, The New York Times Magazine, The American Poetry Review, Ploughshares* and *Best American Poetry.* She has received numerous awards, including the Jessica Nobel-Maxwell Poetry Prize for 1995, given by *American Poetry Review*, the American Academy of Poetry Prize at Syracuse University and the Robert Frost Fellowship in Poetry at the Bread Loaf Writers' Conference. The author of four novels, a book of essays and three collections of poetry, she is a writer-in-residence at Middlebury College in Vermont. When not in Vermont, she and her husband are in the Dominican Republic, where they are part of a small organic coffee farm and literacy center for local farmers. Her poetry collection, *The Woman I Kept to Myself,* was published in 2004 by Algonquin Books of Chapel Hill.

YEHUDA AMICHAI is a well-known Israeli poet who lived in Jerusalem and whose work has been translated into twenty languages. His poem "And the Migration of My Parents" is from the book *Yehuda Amichai: A Life of Poetry 1948–1994*, translated from the Hebrew by Benjamin and Barbara Harshav (Harper Perennial, 1994).

KALPANA ASOK has now lived longer in the United States than in her hometown of Bangalore, India. Her mother tongue is Tamil, but English became her primary language in school. She remembers the day when she began to think in English. She loves her work as a psychotherapist and writer.

W. H. AUDEN needs little introduction. An English poet born in 1907, he later became an American citizen. His poems are among the best-known in the English language. He died in 1973.

RUTH AWAD is a Lebanese-American poet who has received many awards for her work; among them were the 2018 Ohio Book Award for Poetry, a 2016 Ohio Arts Council Individual Excellence Award, the 2012 and 2013 Dorothy Sargent Rosenberg Poetry Prize, and the 2011 *Copper Nickel* Poetry Prize. Her collection, *Set to Music a Wildfire*, was the winner of the 2016 Michael Waters Poetry Prize. Her poem "My Father Dreams of a New Country" is from that book.

JIMMY SANTIAGO BACA is the author of eighteen books of poetry, fiction and non-fiction who has held many Chairs of Distinction and won so many awards it is hard to count them. He founded a non-profit, Cedar Tree, Inc., which supplies free books to libraries and schools on reservations, in barrios, and in inner-city educational centers. He also facilitates writing workshops worldwide for prisons, youth offender facilities, and alternative schools for at-risk youth in many countries. For his work teaching thousands of adults and kids to read and write, the University of New Mexico awarded him an honorary Ph.D.

JAYNE BENJULIAN is the author of *Five Sextillion Atoms* (Saddle Road Press 2016). She began writing as a young girl, leaving letters under the mattress to read years later to see who she had been. Her work appears in numerous literary and professional journals. She was shortlisted for the Bridport Prize in 2017 and a finalist for the James Hearst Poetry Prize from *North American Review* in 2018.

J. PETER BERGMANN is well-known in western Massachusetts as a poet, playwright, actor, and reviewer. He is also Director of Communications at the Herman Melville House in Pittsfield, MA.

SIR JOHN BETJEMAN was Poet Laureate of the U.K. from 1972 until his death in 1984. He used traditional forms and was widely popular because he wrote lightly and nostalgically about serious subjects. Unlike many popular poets, he was also highly regarded by literary critics. The poem in this volume, "False Security," for example, deals with thwarted migration from one social class to another.

RICHARD BLANCO is the fifth presidential inaugural poet in U.S. history—the youngest and first Latino, immigrant, and gay person to serve in such a role. He is the author of several books, including his latest, *How to Love a Country* (Beacon Press, 2019) and *Looking for the Gulf Motel* (University of Pittsburgh Press, 2012). The Academy of American Poets named him Education Ambassador in 2015. He lives in Bethel, Maine.

GWENDOLYN BROOKS was Poet Laureate of the US (a position then called Consultant in Poetry to the Library of Congress), for the 1985-86 term, the first African-American woman to be so honored. In 1976 she had become the first African-American woman inducted into the American Academy of Arts and Letters. But as she says in her poem in this volume, she didn't like to be called by that hyphenated term. "I am BLACK," she says proudly. "Call me by my name."

WITTER BYNNER was born in Brooklyn, New York in 1881. He attended Harvard University, where he met poet Wallace Stevens, who invited him to join the *Harvard Advocate*. After college, he became an editor of *McClure's Magazine* in New York. In the following years he published many books of poems, the first of which was *An Ode to Harvard* in 1907 and received considerable acclaim. In 1922 he and his partner moved to Santa Fe, New Mexico, where they entertained people like Georgia O'Keefe, D.H. Lawrence and Carl Sandburg. Bynner continued publishing poetry for many years, even a collection of *New Poems* in 1960. His work then fell out of favor, to be revived recently by a number of scholars, including James Kraft, whose book, *The Works of Witter Bynner*, brought him renewed, if modest, recognition.

RAFAEL CAMPO is not only a poet and essayist but a Doctor of Internal Medicine, who teaches and practices at Harvard Medical School and Beth Israel Deaconess Medical Center in Boston. Notably, his primary care patients include mostly Latinos, gay/lesbian/bisexual/transgendered people and those with HIV. His awards for poetry include a Guggenheim fellowship, a National Poetry Series award, a Lambda Literary Award, and an honorary Doctor of Literature degree from Amherst College.

MARILYN CHIN, who was born in Hong Kong, grew up in Oregon, U.S. and became a well-known anthologist, translator and educator as well as a poet and novelist. Her work reveals her experience as both an Asian-American and feminist and the difficulties of cultural assimilation. She has won many awards, including the PEN/Josephine Miles Award, a Fulbright Fellowship, a Stegner Fellowship, the Paterson Prize, fellowships from the Radcliffe Institute, the Rockefeller Foundation, the National Endowment for the Arts and a number of Pushcart Prizes. She was featured on Bill Moyers' PBS series, *The Language of Life*, which was edited by one of our co-editors, Jim Haba. Currently, she is a professor emerita at San Diego State University, where she co-directed the MFA program. She has been a Chancellor of the Academy of American Poets since 2018.

LUCILLE CLIFTON, a native of New York State, was born in DePew in 1936, and grew up in Buffalo. She first studied at Howard University, then transferred to and graduated from SUNY Fredonia, in Western New York. Befriended by Ishmael Reed and Langston Hughes, she was first published in Hughes' anthology, *The Poetry of the Negro*, in 1970. Her awards include the Ruth Lilly Poetry Prize, and the University of Massachusetts' Juniper Prize. She was the first author to have two books of poems chosen as finalists for the Pulitzer Prize in one year and then to become another finalist for the Pulitzer in a later year. Poet Laureate of Maryland from 1974–1985, she won the National Book Award for *Blessing the Boats: New and Selected Poems, 1988-2000.* A Distinguished Professor of Humanities at St. Mary's College of Maryland, she was also a Chancellor of the Academy of American Poets. She died in 2010.

PATTY CRANE'S translations of Tomas Tranströmer's poems have appeared in *American Poetry Review, Blackbird, PEN Poetry Series, Poetry Daily, and The New York Times*, among others. BRIGHT SCYTHE, a bilingual selection of her translations, was published by Sarabande Books in 2015.

COUNTEE CULLEN was born in 1903. After the death in 1918 of his paternal grandmother, his guardian, he was taken into the home of the Rev. Frederick A. Cullen, pastor of Harlem's largest congregation, Salem Methodist Episcopal Church. The boy took Cullen's name, and developed cultural awareness under his influence. Frederick A. Cullen was the clergyman who became president of the Harlem chapter of the NAACP. Countee Cullen himself became an important figure in the African-American arts movement that was known as the Harlem Renaissance. In 1928 he was awarded a Guggenheim Fellowship and married the daughter of W.E.B. DuBois, widely acknowledged as leader of the African-American intellectual community. The Poetry Foundation notes that Cullen's poems "powerfully suggest the duality of the black psyche—the simultaneous allegiance to America and rage at her racial inequities."

TOI DERRICOTTE was born in Detroit, Michigan, and has published four collections of poetry: *Natural Birth, The Empress of the Death House, Tender* and *Captivity*— and one work of non-fiction, *The Black Notebooks*. Among her many honors and awards are two fellowships from the National Endowment for the Arts, The United Black Artists, USA, Inc., Distinguished Pioneering of the Arts Award, the Lucille Medwick Memorial Award from the Poetry Society of America, a Pushcart Prize, and the Folger Shakespeare Library Poetry Book Award. Now a professor at the University of Pittsburgh, she was the founder with Cornelius Eady in 1996 of Cave Canem, a workshop retreat for African-American poets.

ALICE DERRY has published five volumes of poetry, the most recent of which are *Hunger* (MoonPath Press, 2018) and *Tremolo* (Red Hen Press, 2012). While still in manuscript, the latter received a 2011 Washington Artist Trust Award. Another of her books, *Strangers To Their Courage* (Louisana State University Press, 2001), was a finalist for the Washington Book Award. She taught English and German at Peninsula College in Port Angeles, Washington, for twenty-nine years, where she co-directed the Foothills Writers' Series. In 2017 she was Writer-in-Residence at Peninsula College.

LORI DESROSIERS' poetry collections are *The Philosopher's Daugher* (Salmon Poetry, 2013) *Sometimes I Hear the Clock Speak* (Salmon Poetry, 2016), and *Keeping Planes in the Air*, (Salmon Poetry, 2016). Two chapbooks, *Inner Sky* and *Typing with e.e. cummings*, are from Glass Lyre Press. Her poems have also appeared in many journals and anthologies, including *Best Indie Lit New England*. A Pushcart Prize nominee, she holds an MFA in Poetry from New England College and teaches Poetry in the Lesley University MFA graduate program. She is also the editor of *Naugatuck River Review*, a journal of narrative poetry, and Wordpeace.co, an online journal dedicated to social justice.

LISKEN VAN PELT DUS teaches writing,, languages and martial arts in western Massachusetts. Her award-winning poetry can be found in many print and online journals, in the anthology, *Climate of Opinion: Sigmund Freud in Poetry*, and in her chapbook, *Everywhere at Once* (Pudding House, 2009) and full-length collection, *What We're Made Of* (Cherry Grove, 2016).

CORNELIUS EADY was born and grew up in Rochester, New York. The author of seven volumes of poetry, he is also known as the co-founder, with Toi Dericotte, of Cave

Canem Foundation, a non-profit organization for black poets. His own poetry is recognized for its down-to-earth language and its concern for peace and justice.

MARTÍN ESPADA'S many books of poems include *Vivas to Those Who Have Failed* (2016), *The Trouble Ball* (2011), *The Republic of Poetry* (2006) and *Alabanza* (2003). He has received the Ruth Lilly Poetry Prize, the Shelley Memorial Award, an Academy of American Poets Fellowship and a Guggenheim Fellowship.

HOWARD FAERSTEIN'S *Dreaming of the Rain in Brooklyn* was published in 2013 by Press 53. A second collection, *Googotz and Other Poems,* came out in September 2018. His work can also be found in numerous print and online journals, including *Great River Review, Rattle, upstreet,* and *Poetry Monday (online)* www. internationalpsychoanalysis.net. He lives in Florence, Massachusetts.

FREDERICK FEIRSTEIN is a practicing psychoanalyst living in New York City. He has been a Guggenheim Fellow in Poetry and twice a Pulitzer Prize nominee. The poem "Mulberry" is from *Fallout* (Word Press, 2008), his eighth full-length collection. His first, *Survivors,* was selected as one of the two outstanding books of 1976 by *Choice.*

CHRIS FOGG is a creative producer, writer, director and dramaturg who has written and directed for the theater for many years, as well as collaborating artistically with choreographers and contemporary dancers. He has written more than thirty works for the stage, as well as four collections of poems, stories and essays, the most recent of which is *Dawn Chorus*, with woodcut illustrations by Chris Waters (Mudlark Press, 2017). Currently, he is at work on a sequence of ten novels set in Manchester, England and called *Ornaments of Grace*. The first and second of these, *Pomona* and *Enclave*, were published in 2019. He lives in Dorset, England.

LINDA NEMEC FOSTER is the author of eleven collections of poetry including *Amber Necklace from Gdansk* (finalist for the Ohio Book Award in Poetry), *Talking Diamonds,* and *The Lake Michigan Mermaid* (2019 Michigan Notable Book). Her work has been published in numerous magazines and journals: e.g. *The Georgia Review, Nimrod, Quarterly West, Witness, New American Writing, North American Review,* and *Verse Daily.* She has received nominations for the Pushcart Prize and awards from the Arts Foundation of Michigan, ArtServe Michigan, National Writer's Voice, Dyer-Ives Foundation, The Poetry Center (NJ), and the Academy of American Poets. From 2003–05, she served as the first Poet Laureate of Grand Rapids, Michigan. Her new book, *The Blue Divide,* will be published in 2021 by New Issues Press. Foster is the founder of the Contemporary Writers Series at Aquinas College.

ROBERT FROST is another poet who needs little introduction. Although widely known as a New England poet especially devoted to New Hampshire, he was born in San Francisco in 1874 and moved to Lawrence,

Massachusetts after his father's death in 1884. His ancestors were New Englanders, so this was a homecoming. His first book was published when he was about 40, but as the years went on he received four Pulitzer Prizes and too many other honors to be listed here. Among the most significant: on his 75th birthday the U.S. Senate passed a resolution in his honor which said, "His poems have helped to guide American thought and humor and wisdom, setting forth in our minds a reliable representation of ourselves and of all men."

SUZANNE GARDINIER was born in New Bedford, Massachusetts, and grew up in Scituate, in the same state. She received a B.A. from the University of Massachusetts and an MFA from Columbia University. She has taught writing at SUNY Old Westbury, Rutgers/Newark, and several other colleges, as well as in the New York City public schools. She now lives in Sag Harbor, New York.

CYNTHIA READ GARDNER's poems have been published in *Alaska Quarterly Review, Southern Poetry Review, The Bridge,* and various anthologies, such as *Crossing Paths: An Anthology of Poems by Women* (Mad River Press, 2002) and *Climate of Opinion: Sigmund Freud in Poetry* (IPBooks, 2017). She has been employed as a clinical social worker for many years and lives in Pittsfield, Massachusetts.

DAVID GIANNINI'S most recent collections of poetry include *In a Moment We May Be Strangely Blended* and *Mayhap* (both from Dos Madres Press in 2019) and *The Rainbow Prepares the Rain* (New Feral Press, 2019) and

Porous Borders (Spuyten Duyvil Press, 2018). He was nominated for a Pushcart Prize in 2015. Awards include: Massachusetts Artist Fellowship Awards; the Osa and Lee Mays Award for Poetry; and award for prosepoetry from the University of Florida, and a 2009 Finalist Award from the *Naugatuck Review.* His work has appeared in international magazines and anthologies.

MARIA MAZZIOTTI GILLAN is the Founder and Executive Director of the Poetry Center at Passaic County Community College in Paterson, New Jersey and editor of the *Paterson Literary Review.* A Bartle Professor and Professor Emerita of English and Creative Writing at Binghamton University-SUNY, she has published more than twenty books of and about poetry and has edited four anthologies. Notably, she also co-edited four anthologies with her daughter Jennifer, including *Unsettling America: Identity lessons, and Growing up Ethnic in America* (Penguin/Putnam). Her numerous awards include the 2014 George Garrett Award for Outstanding Community Service in Literature from AWP; the 2011 Barnes & Noble Writers Award from *Poets & Writers* and the 2008 American Book Award for her book, *All That Lies Between Us (Guernica Editions).*

JIM HABA is the co-editor of this anthology. See About the Editors (p. ix).

BENJAMIN and BARBARA HARSHAW are the two translators from the Hebrew of the poems of Yehuda Amichai, as found in the book, *Yehuda Amichai: A Life of Poetry 1948–1994* (Harper Perennial, 1994).

MARIE HOWE'S books and poems are well-known. Her work has appeared in many magazines, including *The Atlantic, The New Yorker, Harvard Review, Agni* and *The New England Review*. In 2012 she was named Poet Laureate of New York State. Her first book, *The Good Thief*, was selected by Margaret Atwood for the National Poetry Series. She has been a fellow at the Bunting Institute and a recipient of a National Endowment for the Arts fellowship. She teaches at Sarah Lawrence College and New York University and lives in New York City.

T.J. JARRETT is the author of *Zion* (Southern Illinois University Press, 2014) and *Ain't No Grave* (New Issues Press, 2013). She is a software developer in Nashville, Tennessee.

ERICA JONG is a celebrated poet, novelist and essayist, with over thirty published books influential worldwide in languages as diverse as Arabic and Mandarin. Her novel, *Fear of Flying* was her most famous book and gave a big boost to the Women's Movement of the 1970's. Her work has won literary prizes "all over the planet," as her assistant was proud to tell us.

FADY JOUDAH'S most recent poetry collection is *Footnotes in the Order of Disappearance* (Milkweed Editions, 2018). He is a recipient of the Yale Series prize and a Guggenheim fellowship for poetry.

MOJA KAHF was born in Damascus, Syria, moved with her family to the United States in 1971 and grew up in the Midwest. Reviewer Lisa Suhair Majaj commented in *ArteNews* that Kahf's work "draws on American colloquialisms and Quranic suras,…" informed not only by American free verse…but also by a lush energy that draws on the heart of the Arabic oral tradition and Arabic poetry." She is a professor of English at the University of Arkansas.

VASILIKI KATSAROU is the author of the collection *Memento Tsunami* and a chapbook, *Three Sea Stones* (forthcoming). She is editor of two contemporary poetry anthologies published by Ragged Sky Press. A Geraldine R. Dodge poet who teaches at Hunterdon Art Museum in Clinton, New Jersey, she is a Phi Beta Kappa graduate of Harvard University and directed the 35 mm. short film, *Fruitlands 1843*.

JIM KELLEHER has published three books of poems and teaches composition and literature at Northwestern Connecticut Community College. He has worked as a carpenter, public school teacher and poet for his local community. "He once realized his life was a poem," he tells us, "and getting old, he is mostly happy with it."

JANE KENYON published four collections of poems during her short lifetime.She also spent a number of years translating the poems of Anna Akhmatova from Russian into English (published as *Twenty Poems of Anna Akhmatova*, in 1985). She was married to poet Donald Hall and moved with him to his ancestral Eagle Pond Farm in New Hampshire. Many of her poems were based on her life there.

GALWAY KINNELL, born in 1927 in Providence, Rhode Island, died in 2014. He won the Pulitzer Prize for Poetry for his 1982 collection, *Selected Poems* and split the National Book Award for Poetry with Charles Wright. From 1989 to 1993 he was Poet Laureate of Vermont. He was widely appreciated for the spirituality and emotional appeal of his poetry.

KATHLEEN KRAFT is a writer, editor, and yoga teacher. Her chapbook, *Fairview Road*, was published by Finishing Line Press and her work has appeared in many journals, including *Five Points, Sugar House Review, Gargoyle,* and *The Satirist.* She lives in the Berkshires, MA.

TED KOOSER is a Pulitzer Prize-winner and the thirteenth Poet Laureate of the United States. His plain-spoken poems are widely popular, and for good reason. Born in Ames, Iowa in 1939, he taught for many years at the University of Nebraska at Lincoln. He told reviewers that he wrote for an hour and a half every morning before work. By the time he retired he had published seven books of poetry.

LAVINIA KUMAR's books are *The Celtic Fisherman's Wife: A Druid Life* (2017); *The Skin and Under* (Word Tech, 2015). She has also published three chapbooks: *Beauty, Salon, Art* (Desert Williw Press, 2019); *Let There Be Color* (Lives You Touch Publications, 2016), and *River of Saris* (Main Street Rag, 2013). She publishes in U.S., Irish & UK publications.

DANUSHA LAMERIS is Poet Laureate of Santa Cruz, California. Her new book, *Bonfire Opera*, is forthcoming from the University of Pittsburgh, Press.

EMMA LAZARUS' poem "The New Colossus" was written in 1883 and is now engraved on the Statue of Liberty that stands in New York Harbor.

MIHAELA MOSCALIUC is the author of two poetry collections, *Father Dirt* (Alice James Books, 2010) and *Immigrant Model* (University of Pittsburgh Press, 2015), translator of Carmelia Leonte's *The Hiss of the Viper* (Carnegie Mellon UP, 2014) and Liliana Ursu's *Clay and Star* (Etruscan Press, 2019), editor of *Insane Devotion: On the Writing of Gerald Stern* (U of Trinity P, 2016), and co-editor of *Border Lines* (Knopf, 2020). She is associate professor at Monmouth University, New Jersey.

MARILYN NELSON is the former Poet Laureate of Connecticut. Born in Cleveland, Ohio into a military family, she is the daughter of one of the last of the famed Tuskegee Airmen. A three-time finalist for the National Book Award, she is the author or translator of seventeen poetry collections, as well as many collections of verse for children. Her awards include a John Newbery Medal, the Poets' Prize, the Ruth Lilly Poetry Prize, the Frost Medal, and the NSK Neustadt Prize for Children's Poetry.

NAOMI SHIHAB NYE is the poet who selects the poems you see every Sunday in the *New York Times Sunday Magazine*.

The daughter of a Palestinian father and American mother, she was born in St. Louis, Missouri but lived during her high school years in a variety of places: Ramallah in Palestine; the Old City in Jerusalem, and San Antonio, Texas. She received a B.A. in English and world religions from Trinity University. She is the author of numerous books of poems, the most recent of which is *The Tiny Journalist* (BOA Editions, 2019), as well as several books of poetry and fiction for children, and received a Jane Addams Children's Book award in 1988. Other honors include awards from the International Poetry Forum and the Texas Institute of Letters, the Carity Randall Prize and four Pushcart Prizes. She has been a Lannan Fellow, a Guggenheim Fellow, and a Witter Bynner Fellow. In 1988 she received the Academy of American Poets Lavan Award, judged by W.S. Merwin. Nye served as a Chancellor of the Academy of American Poets from 2010–2015 and is currently the Poetry Foundation's Young People's Poet Laureate, a position she will hold until 2021, during which time she will continue to select the fine poems we see in our Sunday *Times*. Many other honors and awards have come her way—too many for your editors to list here, much as they love her work.

SHARON OLDS, author of five poetry collections, most recently *Odes* (Penguin/Random House, 2016), has been the recipient of the 2013 Pulitzer Prize for Poetry, the 1984 National Book Critics Circle Award, and the first San Francisco Poetry Center Award in 1980. Born in San Francisco, she grew up in Berkeley, California, where she was raised. She teaches creative writing at New York

University. Her work is known for its often erotic imagery and its close examination of family relationshps.

ALICIA SUSKIN OSTRIKER is well-known as a poet, critic, scholar and activist. Born in Brooklyn, New York, she lived for many years in Princeton, New Jersey, and recently moved to the city again, this time to Manhattan. She has won many prizes for her work, including the Berru Award from the Jewish Book Council and the Jewish National Book Award. In 2015 she was elected a Chancellor of the Academy of American Poets, and in 2018 was named the New York State Poet Laureate. She has also been a finalist for both the National Book Award and the Lenore Marshall Poetry Prize. She teaches in the Drew University low-residency MFA program in poetry.

ANNE PORTER: 1911–2011. Those dates are not an accident. She died at 100, and her first collection, *An Altogether Different Language*, published when she was 83, was a finalist for the National Book Award. She was quoted in an interview as saying, "People don't use their creativity as they get older. They think this is supposed to be the end of this and the end of that. But you can't always be sure that it is the end." She published a second collection: *Living Things: Collected Poems* in 2006. Her work has been anthologized in the *Oxford Book of American Poetry* (2oo6). Long before she first appeared in print, however, she had been writing poetry. Married to the painter Fairfield Porter, she raised five children. It wasn't until her husband died that she decided to take her poetry seriously.

LEROY V. QUINTANA was born in Albuquerque, New Mexico. He is not only a poet, author, editor and retired professor but a Vietnam Veteran who served in the Army Airborne and a Long Range Reconnaissance Patrol unit in 1967–68. His work has appeared in numerous journals and anthologies, and he has twice received an American Book Award, one in 1982 for *Paper Dance* and another in 1993 for *The History of Home.* Other awards include one from the El Paso Border Regional Library Association. He studied psychiatry at Western New Mexico University and in 1984 received an M.A. in counseling.

ZARA RAAB grew up in northern California, where her family had lived for 200 years. She now lives in Massachusetts, north of Boston. Her poems and reviews have appeared in many literary magazines, including *The Hudson Review,* and she has published five collections of poetry, the most recent of which is *Fracas and Asylum* (David Robert Books, 2013).

ADRIENNE RICH, who was born in Baltimore, Maryland in 1929, became one of America's most influential poets, especially to women and on their behalf. Both "out" and outspoken, she was called, as one critic put it, "a poet of towering reputation and towering rage." The year she graduated from Radcliffe College in 1951 she was selected by W.H. Auden for the Yale Series of Younger Poets prize for her book *A Change of World* (Yale University Press, 1951). Her career took off after that, and she went on to write more books, both poetry and essays, and to receive more awards, notably the National Book Award, for "Diving into the Wreck" (1971), which she accepted with Alice Walker and Audre Lorde "in the name of all women who have been silenced in literary culture." She became a Chancellor of the Academy of American Poets and received many other awards, including the prestigious Bollingen Prize for Poetry in 2003.

ALBERTO RIOS is another highly-honored poet. He was the inaugural Poet Laureate of the State of Arizona, a position he held from 2013-2015, has been a Chancellor of the Academy of American Poets and is a Professor of English at Arizona State University. Born in Nogales, Arizona, along the border of Mexico and with a Mexican father, this background has been a strong influence on his poems and short-stories. The author of ten books and chapbooks of poetry, he has been the recipient of a Walt Whitman award and nominated for a National Book Award for poetry.

TRACY K. SMITH was born in Falmouth Massachusetts in 1972 and raised in Fairfield, California. She has been a prize-winner from the beginning, with four acclaimed poetry collections, and in 2017 was named Poet Laureate of the United States. She studied at Harvard University, where she was a member of the "Dark Room Collective," a reading series for writers of color, and then went on to Columbia University for a Master of Fine Arts. Her first collection, *The Body's Question,* won the Cave Canem Poetry Prize in 2002; her second, *Duende,* won the 2006 James Laughlin Award from the Academy of American Poets. Her collection, *Life on Mars,* won the 2012 Pulitzer Prize for Poetry. She also edited the anthology *American Journal: Fifty Poems for Our Time*, published by Graywolf Press, as were all her other books. *Wade in the Water* (Graywolf, 2018), won the 2019 Anisfield-Wolf Book Award in Poetry and was shortlisted for the 2018 T.S. Eliot Prize. She lives in New Jersey and has been the director of Princeton University's creative writing program.

MARK SMITH-SOTO is a Costa Rican American poet, playwright and Professor of Spanish and Latin-American literature at the University of North Carolina at Greensboro. For over twenty years he has also edited *International Poetry Review* at that university. The author of three books of poetry, his poems have also appeared in many journals, such as *Nimrod, Carolina Quarterly, Literary Review, Americas Review* and *Kenyon Review*. His awards include a fellowship in creative writing from the National Endowment for the Arts; North Carolina Writers' Network's Persephone Competition prize for his chapbook, *Green Mango Collage* and their Randall Jarrell-Harperprints Poetry Competion prize for his chapbook, *Shafts*.

GARY SNYDER is best known and remembered as a member of the "beat generation" of poets and writers and the San Francisco Renaissance and also for his spirituality. Like most of those in this volume, he has published many works of poetry and prose and received numerous awards. Among the latter are an American Academy of Arts and Letters award, the Bollingen Prize, a Guggenheim Foundation fellowhip, the Bess Hokin Prize and the Levinson Prize from *Poetry,* an American Book Award, a Pulitzer Prize, the Robert Kirsch Lifetime Achievement Award from the *Los Angeles Times*, the Ruth Lilly Poetry Prize, and the Shelley Memorial Award. In 2003 he was elected a Chancellor of the Academy of American Poets. The Academy also gave him the 2012 Wallace Stevens Award for lifetime achievement. He is still listed as a Professor of English at the University of California, Davis.

WILLIAM STAFFORD, who died in 1993, was born in Hutchinson, Kansas, in 1914 and widely celebrated throughout his life. He has been called a "witness for peace and for honesty," recognizing in his writing that "justice will take us millions of intricate moves." Author of over fifty books and recipient of a National Book Award for *Traveling through the Dark,* he was a professor at Lewis & Clark College, but taught elsewhere, throughout the world. Poet Laureate of the United States in 1970 when it was still called "Consultant in Poetry to the Library of Congress," he became Oregon's Poet Laureate in 1975. *The Way It Is: New and Selected Poems* (Graywolf, 1998) is a generous selection of his poems, including unpublished poems from his last year, including one he wrote the day he died. It has a preface from Naomi Shihab Nye.

A.E. STALLINGS, whose most recent book is *Like* (Farrar, Straus & Giroux, 2018), is an American poet born in Decatur, Georgia, who has lived in Athens, Greece since 1999. The author of three books of poetry, she has won many awards, including the 2008 Poets Prize, a MacArthur

Fellowship, the Richard Wilbur Award and a Guggenheim Fellowship for Creative Arts. Her collection *Like* was a finalist for a Pulitzer Prize. She is a frequent contributor of essays and reviews to *The American Scholar, Parnassus, Poetry Review, the Times Literary Supplement* and *The Yale Review.*

HOWARD F. STEIN is, by profession, a medical and psychoanalyst anthropologist and psychohistorian. He is the author of many books and articles in these and related fields. His book, *Developmental Time, Cultural Space* (University of Oklahoma Press, 1987), reinforced the thinking of the editors about migration and immigration.

GERALD STERN exemplifies everything this anthology is about. He is the son of Eastern European immigrants, a frequent topic of his unique poems, together with his working-class background. At the same time, he is cosmopolitan in outlook. Afraid of nothing, he speaks of everything, often with humor and always with wit. There is no one like him.A founder of the MFA program at New England College, which has since become the low-residency MFA Program in Poetry at Drew University in New Jersey, he remains a kind of guru to budding poets everywhere. His many honors include the Wallace Stevens Award, the Bess Hokin Award, the Ruth Lilly Prize, the Bernard F. Conners Award from *The Paris Review,* and the Pennsylvania Governor's Award for Excellence in the Arts, and fellowships from the Pennsylvania Council on the Arts, the National Endowment for the Arts, and the Guggenheim Foundation. From 2000–2002, he was Poet Laureate of New Jersey.

SEKOU SUNDIATA It's hard to believe we're writing in the past tense about someone who was born in 1948. This unclassifiable African-American musician and multi-genre writer and performer died in 2007. Before he ever published a book of poems, he taught at the New School in New York City, where he was their first Writer-in-Residence. In 2003 he toured the United States, performing his one-man theatrical piece, *Blessing the Boats,* which combined monologues, readings, stand-up comedy and spoken word and storytelling with recorded music and video. Many readers and television viewers may recall his appearance with Bill Moyers, who featured him in the PBS series on poetry, *The Language of Life.*

TOMAS GOSTA TRANSTRÖMER, who was born in Stockholm, Sweden in 1931 and died in 2015, was a writer, poet and translator whose poems have been translated into over sixty languages. Considered one of the most important European and Scandinavian writers since World War II, he is praised for work that is accessible, even in translation. In 2011 he was awarded the Nobel Prize in Literature.

CHARLOTTE GOULD WARREN's *Dangerous Bodies* (SFA Press, Texas), and *Gandhi's Lap*, Washington Prize winner (*Word Works*, Washington, D.C.) explore themes central to her memoir, *Jumna: Sacred River* (SFA Press), which chronicles her childhood in India and her coming of age in the United States during the turbulent sixties.

CHRIS WATERS lives and works in Devon, U.K.—but identifies as a European! (Exclamation point is his!). He has published three poetry collections—*Arisaig; Through a Glass, Lately;* and most recently *Dancing Satyr.* He is also a musician and spoken-word performer, enjoying working with fellow performers on collaborative shows and events. His work has won several prizes in the U.K.

MICHAEL WATERS is the author of thirteen books of poems, including *Caw* (BOA Editions, 2020), *The Dean of Discipline* (University of Pittsburgh Press, 2018), & *Celestial Joyride* (BOA Editions, 2016), & co-editor of several anthologies, including *Border Lines* (Knopf, 2020), *Reel Verse* (Knopf, 2019), & *Contemporary American Poetry* (Houghton Mifflin, 2006). *Darling Vulgarity* (BOA, 2006) was a finalist for the *Los Angeles Times* Book Prize & *Parthenopi: New and Selected Poems* (BOA, 2006) was a finalist for the Paterson Poetry Prize. His poems have appeared in numerous journals, including *Poetry, Paris Review, Yale Review, Kenyon Review, North American Review, Rolling Stone* & *American Poetry Review.* A 2017 Guggenheim Fellow & 2007 Fulbright Fellow, recipient of five Pushcart Prizes, & fellowships from the National Endowment for the Arts & NJ State Council on the Arts, Waters lives without a cell phone in Ocean, NJ.

HILDE WEISERT is a scholar and events coordinator as well as a poet. Her 2015 poetry collection, *The Scheme of Things,* with cover art by Jim Haba, was published by David Robert Books. Her poems have also appeared in many literary magazines, including *Ms., The Cincinnati Review, The Cortland Review, Prairie Schooner, The Sun, Southern Poetry Review,* and *Lips.* In fall 2019 her essay, "Randall Jarrell and Adrienne Rich: A Found Guide to Mutual Admiration" was published in *Hudson Review.* Awards for her poetry include the 2017 Gretchen Warren Award from the New England Poetry Club, the *Tifferet Journal* Poetry Award and the 2008 Lois Cranston Poetry Award. For many years she worked as a Dodge poet at the famous Dodge Poetry Festival in New Jersey. She organizes many events for the Sandisfield Arts Center in Berkshire County, Massachusetts, of which she is co-president.

IRENE WILLIS is, with Jim Haba, co-editor of this anthology. (See About the Editors, p. viii).

NINA ISRAEL ZUCKER is both a poet and teacher. She has taught creative writing at Rowan University, participated in the Geraldine R. Dodge Poetry Festival, facilitated the Spring/Fountain poetry for educators throughout New Jersey, and is a teacher for elementary English language learners in Cherry Hill, New Jersey. Her work has appeared in the anthology, *Poets Against the War,* edited by Sam Hamill (Copper Canyon Press), *US 1 Worksheets, 30/30 poets* for Tupelo Press, and many other publications.

Acknowledgments

Grateful acknowledgment is made to the American Psychoanalytic Association, without whose generous support this book would not be possible. We are also grateful to the many individual poets, publications and publishers who have made their work available to us without fee, because of the importance of this project. Psycho-geographer Howard F. Stein also contributed valuable insights.

Ahren, Justen: "Detained" from *A Machine for Remembering* (by Justen Ahren) Reprinted here by permission of the poet.

Alvarez, Julia: "Spic" from *The Woman I Kept to Myself* (Algonquin Books of Chapel Hill, 2004)

Amichai, Yehuda: "And the Migration of My Parents" and "The Diameter of the Bomb" from *Yehuda Amichai: A Life of Poetry 1948–1994* (Harper Perennial, 1995)

Asok, Kalpana: "Raw" from *Everyday Flowers* (IPBooks, 2018).

Auden, W. H.: "Refugee Blues" was written in September 1939, as part of a long piece called "Ten Songs" from *W.H. Auden: Collected Poems*, edited by Edward Mendelson (Random House Modern Library, 2007)

Awad, Ruth: "My Father Dreams of a New Country" from *Set to Music a Wildfire* (Southern Indiana Review Press, 2018)

Baca, Jimmy Santiago: "The Day I Am Freed" from *When I Walk Through That Door, I Am* (Beacon Press, 2019).

Benjulian, Jayne: "Wedding Dress" Permission of the poet.

Bergman, J. Peter: "Provenance" Permission of the poet.

Betjeman, Sir John: "False Security" from *Collected Poems of John Betjeman* (Hougton Mifflin, 1971).

Blanco, Richard: "Mother Country" from *How to Love a Country* (Beacon Press, 2019

Brooks, Gwendolyn: "I Am a Black" from *The Essential Gwendolyn Brooks, edited by Elizabeth Alexander* (American Poets Project: The Library of America, 2005).

Bynner, Witter: "The Wall" and "Defeat" from *The Selected Witter Bynner* edited by James Kraft (University of New Mexico Press, 1995

Campo, Rafael: "In English That Is Spanish" from *What the Body Told* (Duke University Press, 1996)

Chin, Marilyn: "We Are Americans Now, We Live in the Tundra" and "Floral Apron" from the *The Phoenix Gone, The Terrace Empty* (Milkweed Editions, 1993).

Clifton, Lucille: "Sorrow Song" from *Blessing the Boats: New and Selected Poems 1988–2000* (BOA Editions, Ltd.2000)

Cullen, Countee: "Incident" from *Color*, his first book, published in 1925 and reprinted in *Countee Cullen: Collected Poems* (American Poets Project #32)

Derricotte, Toi: "Passing" and "Workshop on Racism" from *Tender* (University of Pittsburgh Press, 1997). Reprinted by permission of the poet.

Derry, Alice : "When the Outside Is Completely Dark" Permission of the poet.

Desrosiers, Lori: "Ashkenazy" from *Sometimes I Hear the Clock Speak*" (Salmon Poetry, 2016). Reprinted here by permission of the poet.

Dus, Lisken Van Pelt: "My Father Asks What I Remember" and "Kwashiorkor" Permission of the poet.

Eady, Cornelius: "A Little Bit of Soap" from *You Don't Miss Your Water* (Henry Holt & Co., 1995). Reprinted here by permission of the poet..

Espada, Martín: "Bully" "Jorge the Church Janitor Finally Quits" and "Ode to the Soccer Balls Sailing Over a Barbed-Wire Fence" from *Alabanza: New and Selected Poems*: 1982–2002 (W.W.Norton & Co., 2003). Reprinted here by permission of the poet.

Faerstein, Howard: "The Baby in the Boat" from *Dreaming of the Rain in Brooklyn* (Press 53 LLC, 2013); "Morris" and "Godmother Goldie" from *Googotz and Other Poems* (Press 53 LLC, 2018). Reprinted here by permission of the poet.

Feirstein, Frederick: "Mulberry Street" from *Fallout* (Word Press, 2008)—Reprinted here by permission of the poet.

Fogg, Chris: "Ladybirds" from *Painting by Numbers* (Mudlark Press, 2017). Reprinted here by permission of the poet.

Foster, Linda Nemec: "Memories of an Immigrant Childhood" from *Paterson Literary Review* (Issue 47, 2019). Reprinted here by permission of the editor.

Frost, Robert: "Mending Wall" from *The Poetry of Robert Frost: The Collected Poems,* Edited by Edward Connery Lathem (Henry Holt & Co., 1979).

Gardinier, Suzanne: "Refugees" from *The New World* (University of Pittsburgh Press, 1993).

Gardner, Cynthia Read: "Haiti after the Flood"— Permission of the poet.

Giannini, David: "Eatery" from *In a Moment We May Be Strangely Blended* (Dos Madres, 2019) and *Tikkun Olam* (Repairing the World) from a new manuscript. Both poems are reprinted here by permission of the poet.

Gillan, Maria Mazziotti: "I Was the Girl Who Never Spoke" from *Ancestors' Song* (Bordighera Press, 2013) .

Haba, Jim: "What They Bring" and "These Angels" are both reprinted here by permission of the poet.

Howe, Marie: "Sixth Grade" from *What the Living Do* (W.W. Norton & Co., 1998).

Jarrett, T. J. : "Fort Comfort" from *Poetry* (May 2019).

Jong, Erica: "Child on the Beach" from *The World Began with Yes* (Red Hen Press, 2019); reprinted here by permission of the poet.

Joudah, Fady: "Dehiscence" from *The Baffler* (No. 43, Jan./Feb. 2019).

Kahf, Moja: "My Grandmother Washes Her Feet in the Bathroom at Sears" from *E-mails from Scheharazad* (University Press of Florida, 2003).

Katsarou, Vasiliki : "Father Tongue" from, *Memento Tsunami* (Ragged Sky Press, 2011). Reprinted here by permission of the poet.

Kelleher, Jim: "I Worry How I Appear before God" – Permission of the poet.

Kenyon, Jane: "Here" from *Constance* and in her *Collected Poems* (Graywolf Press, 2005).

Kinnell, Galway: "Prayer" from *A New Selected Poems, Edited by S.M. Inrator and M. Scribner* (HarperCollins, 1995).

Kraft, Kathleen: "Swedish Fish" First published in *Gemini Magazine*. Reprinted here by permission of the poet.

Kooser, Ted: "At Nightfall" and "The Great-Grandparents" from *Kindest Regards: New and Selected Poems* (Copper Canyon Press, 2018).

Kumar, Lavinia: "Refugees Near Calais, France" –Permission of the poet.

Lally, Michael: "It Takes One to Know One" from *Another Way to Play: Poems 1960–2017)* (Seven Stories Press, 2018).

Lameris, Danusha: "Small Kindnesses" from *The New York Times Sunday Magazine* (September 9, 2019). Reprinted here by permission of the poet.

Lazarus, Emma: "The New Colossus" was written in 1883. It is engraved on the Statue of Liberty in New York Harbor.

Lee, Li-Young: "The Cleaving" from *The City in Which I Love You* (BOA Editions, Ltd., 1990).

Merwin, W. S. : "Émigré" from *Migration: New and Selected Poems* (Copper Canyon Press, 2005).

Moscaliuc, Mihaela: "Refugee Song" from *Immigrant Model* (University of Pittsburgh Press, 2015). Reprinted here by permission of the poet.

Nelson, Marilyn: "Minor Miracle" from *The Fields of Praise: New and Selected Poems,* (Louisiana State University Press, 1997).

Olds, Sharon: "Secondary Boycott Ode" from *Odes* (Random House, 2016).

Ostriker, Alicia Suskin: "Ghazal: America the Beautiful" and "Ghazal: America" from *Waiting for the Light* (University of Pittsburgh Press, 2017). Reprinted here by permission of the poet.

Porter, Anne: "Susanna"—from *Living Things.* Permission of Steerforth Press.

Quintana, Leroy V.: "What It Was Like" from *The Great Whirl of Exile"* (Curbstone Press, 1999).

Raab, Zara "Migrations" from *The Hudson Review* (Vol. LXX No. 4 Winter 2018). Reprinted here by permission of the poet.

Rich, Adrienne: "Prospective Immigrants Please Note" from-*Snapshots of a Daughter-in-Law*" (HarperCollins, 1963).

Rios, Alberto: "A House Called Tomorrow" Reprinted here by permission of the poet.

Smith, Tracy K.: The United States Welcomes You" from *Wade in the Water* (Graywolf Press, 2018).

Smith–Soto, Mark "Accent" from *The Sun* (April 2019). Reprinted here by permission of the poet.

Snyder, Gary: "How Poetry Comes to Me" from *No Nature, 1992.*

Stafford, William: "The Little Girl by the Fence at School" from *The Way It Is: New and Selected Poems* (Graywolf Press, 1998) and "Pretend You Live in a Room" from *Even in Quiet Places* (Confluence Press, 1997).

Stallings, A. E.: "Refugee Fugue" from *Like* (Farrar, Straus Giroux, 2018).

Stein, Howard F. "Refugees" and "Unclaimed" by permission of the poet.

Stern, Gerald: "The Dancing" from *This Time: New and Selected Poems (W. W. Norton & Co., 1998).*

Sundiata, Sekou: "Blink Your Eyes" from *Sekou Sundiata Revisited* (Mapp International, 2013).

Tranströmer, Tomas "Romanesque Arches" from *Bright Scythe.* Permission of Patty Crane, translator.

Warren, Charlotte Gould "A Girl Tying Ribbons in Her Hair" and "Walking to School"—Permission of the poet.

Waters, Chris "Field Notes"—Permission of the poet.

Waters, Michael: "Sophie Rose" from *The Dean of Discipline* (University of Pittsburgh Press, 2018) and "The Bicycle" from *Anniversary of the Air"* (Carnegie Mellon University Press, 1985). Reprinted here by permission of the poet.

Weisert, Hilde: "The Transit Hall on Pier 86." Permission of the poet.

Willis, Irene—"Border" Permission of the poet; "The Secret at the Back of the Cupboard" from *Marsh Hawk Review.* Reprinted here by permission of the poet.

Zucker, Nina Israel—"Refugee in Suburbia" and "Watar/Homeland" Permission of the poet.

Special gratitude also to Ernie Lowell, Computer Consultant *extraordinaire*, Olivia VanSant, wonderful P.A., Chris Fogg, U.K., for his constant support, and beloved canine, Abigail, who was here for the beginning of this and all through the previous anthology and for *Rehearsal*, poems by Irene Willis.